Just a Grammar Workbook
Middle Grades

J. Impecoven, et al.
1st Edition © 2021

EDITOR'S NOTE: This book is designed as a compliment to a live or online course in English grammar. It contains practice and exercises for a variety of topics, but there are no lessons or instruction of any kind. Space is provided for notes so that each educator can convey the necessary concepts in their own way.

Just a Grammar Workbook - Middle Grades may not be reproduced for distribution of any kind, electronically or in print. Reproduction for any commercial use is forbidden. Copyrighted Material. All rights reserved.

Table of Contents

1. Grammar Basics (Review)
   - Nouns, Verbs   8
   - Adjectives, Adverbs   9
   - Pronouns   10
2. Sentences
   - Subject/Verb Agreement   11
   - NOTES   13
   - Subject/ Predicate   14
   - Clauses – Independent/Dependent   15
   - NOTES   18
   - Simple/Compound Sentences   20
   - NOTES   22
   - LIST of Subordinating Conjunctions   23
   - Complex/Compound-Complex   24
   - NOTES   28
   - Sentence Types   29
3. Prepositions
   - LIST of Prepositions   31
   - NOTES   32
   - Prepositions and Prepositional Phrases   34
4. Compounds
   - Subjects and Verbs   40
   - Objects of Prepositions   42
5. Nouns
   - NOTES   44
   - Common/Proper   45
   - Concrete/Abstract   47
   - Subjects and Objects   49
   - Pronouns (intro)   50
6. Adjectives
   - NOTES   51

Table of Contents (2)

- Descriptive Adjectives	52
- NOTES	56
- Limiting Adjectives (Noun Determiners)	57
- NOTES	63
- Predicate Adjectives	64

7. Verbs

- NOTES	68
- Verb Tenses (Past, Present, Future)	69
- NOTES	72
- Action Verbs/Linking Verbs	73
- NOTES	77
- Predicate Adjectives	78
- Predicate Nominatives	79
- NOTES	83
- Transitive Verbs/Intransitive Verbs	84
- Direct Objects	86
- NOTES	88
- Indirect Objects	89
- LIST of Helping (Auxiliary) Verbs	93
- NOTES	94
- Helping Verbs and Verb Phrases	96
- Infinitives	101
- NOTES	102
- Contractions	103
- NOTES	107
- Irregular Past Tense	108
- Irregular Past Participle	110

8. Adverbs

- NOTES	112
- Descriptive ("How") Adverbs	113
- NOTES	117

Table of Contents (3)

- "When" Adverbs	119
- "Where" Adverbs	122
- "To What Extent" Adverbs	125
9. Pronouns	
- NOTES	129
- Nominative (Subjective) Pronouns	131
- Objective Pronouns	134
- NOTES	137
- Possessive Pronouns	138
- Reflexive Pronouns	141
- Pronoun or Adjective?	142
10. Appositives	
- NOTES	143
- Appositives	144
11. Verbals	
- NOTES	148
- Verbals	149

Basics
Nouns and Verbs

A. Directions: In the following sentences, circle any <u>noun</u>.

1. My new car drives quickly down the street.

2. Miguel wrote it carefully with a mechanical pencil.

3. He and she are moving silently across the shiny dance floor.

4. Her silly dog ran clumsily near the pool and fell in.

B. Directions: In the following sentences, circle any <u>verb</u>.

1. My new car drives quickly down the street.

2. Miguel wrote it carefully with a mechanical pencil.

3. He and she are moving silently across the shiny dance floor.

4. Her silly dog ran clumsily near the pool and fell in.

C. Directions: In the following blanks, write five <u>nouns</u> in the first column and five <u>verbs</u> in the second column.

<u>Nouns</u>   <u>Verbs</u>

1. _____   1. _____

2. _____   2. _____

3. _____   3. _____

4. _____   4. _____

5. _____   5. _____

Basics
Adjectives and Adverbs

A. Directions: In the following sentences, circle any <u>adjective</u>.

1. My new car drives quickly down the street.
2. Miguel wrote it carefully with a mechanical pencil.
3. He and she are moving silently across the shiny dance floor.
4. Her silly dog ran clumsily near the pool and fell in.

B. Directions: In the following sentences, circle any <u>adverb</u>.

1. My new car drives quickly down the street.
2. Miguel wrote it carefully with a mechanical pencil.
3. He and she are moving silently across the shiny dance floor.
4. Her silly dog ran clumsily near the pool and fell in.

C. Directions: In the following blanks, write five <u>adjectives</u> in the first column and five <u>adverbs</u> in the second column.

<u>Adjectives</u>   <u>Adverbs</u>

1. _____   1. _____
2. _____   2. _____
3. _____   3. _____
4. _____   4. _____
5. _____   5. _____

Basics
Pronouns

A. Directions: In the following sentences, circle any pronoun.

1. My new car drives quickly down the street.

2. Miguel wrote it carefully with a mechanical pencil.

3. He and she are moving silently across the shiny dance floor.

4. Her silly dog ran clumsily near the pool and fell in.

5. Can you hand me the coat beside them?

6. I brought us to our vacation rental.

7. Who loaned me their butterfly net?

B. Directions: Write any pronoun that makes sense into the blanks to complete each of the following sentences.

1. _____ flies rockets to moons.

2. Margaret takes _____ to the skating rink.

3. The mighty oak tree lives near _____.

4. My mom and _____ walk dogs together.

5. _____ house is on the next block.

6. _____ am the only one in the car.

7. Those dinosaurs loaned _____ an umbrella.

8. Some of the students want to go with _____.

Sentences
Subject/Verb Agreement

A. Directions: In the following sentences, circle the subject that agrees with the verb in the sentence.

1. The dog (chase / chases) the school bus.

2. Our grandparents (operate / operates) a bed and breakfast.

3. I (are / am) the fastest runner at my college.

4. They (call / calls) their parents on Sundays.

5. Steve and Keira (jump / jumps) on the trampoline.

6. President Ichabod Worthington (sleep / sleeps) in a hammock.

7. We (drive / drives) to the coast in the summer.

B. Directions: In the following sentences, circle the correct form of the verb that agrees with the subject of the sentence.

1. The old (man / men) go to the park in the afternoon.

2. (They / He) wants the burrito without cheese.

3. Our (cat / cats) sleeps in the loft of the barn.

4. My new (toy / toys) are in the backyard.

5. A (sailor / sailors) sails the seven seas.

6. Some sneaky (fox / foxes) follow us home after tea.

7. (I , Me) am the apprentice to the blacksmith.

Sentences
Subject/Verb Agreement

A. Directions: In the following sentences, write a <u>subject</u> in the blank that agrees with the <u>verb</u> in the sentence.

1. Her red _____ sits in the hallway.

2. The _____ run quickly through the field.

3. _____ screams at the moon.

4. Our _____ seem very hungry.

5. Their seven _____ live in Louisiana.

6. _____ read a lot of books.

7. A _____ crawls across the back porch.

B. Directions: In the following sentences, write the correct present tense form of any <u>verb</u> that agrees with the <u>subject</u> of the sentence.

1. Those alligators _____ in the swamp.

2. My bike _____ very slowly with a flat tire.

3. I _____ a hard worker.

4. Miguel and Rava _____ to the pool daily.

5. We _____ trees in the jungle.

6. His grandfather _____ a hat with a feather.

7. Several aggressive monkeys _____ our lunch.

Sentences/Clauses
NOTES

Subject and Predicate

A. Directions: Draw a line between the complete subject and the complete predicate.

   Example: The dog runs away. → The dog / runs away.

1. A doctor studied hard.
2. The monkeys eat bananas.
3. Bob sells car insurance.
4. A donkey will eat anything.
5. Lucy goes to the store.
6. Tiny dinosaurs drive tiny cars.
7. Our mechanic will be fast.
8. Ms. Nham reads scary stories.
9. The hungry dragon ate a lot.
10. My gray cat sleeps in trees.

B. Directions: Draw a line under the simple subject and two lines under the verb.

   Example: The dog runs away. → The dog runs away.

1. A doctor studied hard.
2. The monkeys eat bananas.
3. Bob sells car insurance.
4. A donkey will eat anything.
5. Lucy goes to the store.
6. Tiny dinosaurs drive tiny cars.
7. Our mechanic will be fast.
8. Ms. Nham reads scary stories.
9. The hungry dragon ate a lot.
10. My gray cat sleeps in trees.

Clauses
Independent/Dependent

A. Directions: Read the <u>clauses</u> below. Underline the <u>simple subject</u> once and the <u>verbs</u> twice. If the clause is an <u>independent clause</u>, write an <u>I</u> in the blank.

Examples: ___ When the man arrives ➔ ___ When the <u>man</u> <u>arrives</u>
___ The dog runs fast ➔ <u>I</u> The <u>dog</u> <u>runs</u> fast

1. ____ My bike was not expensive

2. ____ Until the sun sets

3. ____ She won

4. ____ Since I don't have a car

5. ____ Than his classmates can

6. ____ The cheetah runs quickly

7. ____ We wanted to go

8. ____ If you can play on Monday

9. ____ Bears are hungry

10. ____ Before your dinner gets cold

11. ____ That store is closed

12. ____ Although she didn't win

13. ____ A baseball rolled away

14. ____ Our team won

15. ____ While Maya's dog ran

Clauses
Independent/Dependent

A. Directions: Each of the following are <u>dependent clauses</u>. Write an <u>independent clause</u> in each of the blanks to form a complete sentence.

Examples: _____ unless we can fix it. ➔
<u> We can't take our car </u> unless we can fix it.

1. _____ if dinner is ready.

2. Whenever you visit _____.

3. _____ even though you ate pie.

4. Because you are so tall, _____.

5. After he sold all of his collectables, _____.

6. _____, now that the rocket is in orbit.

7. _____ whether the storm arrives or not.

8. Although she made it to the audition, _____.

9. _____ if only she saw them leave.

10. Now that the bears are gone, _____.

11. When the tide comes in at the beach, _____.

12. Even if the monkeys sign the truce, _____.

13. _____ as soon as the monsters eat.

14. Supposing the snakes are asleep, _____?

15. While Maya's dog ran, _____.

Clauses
Independent/Dependent

A. Directions: In the following sentences, underline the <u>independent clauses</u>.

Examples: If the driver is late, we will walk. →

If the driver is late, <u>we will walk</u>.

1. I received a good grade because I studied often.

2. Now that the cows are in the stable, we can eat dinner.

3. Their big hungry rabbit ate every carrot in the house.

4. Since they took the car, the children must walk home.

5. The bomb will explode unless we diffuse it.

6. Our rooster ran away from home whether you like it or not.

7. Before the alarm sounds, you need to complete the puzzle.

8. His cat will run in here as soon as she hears the can opener.

9. Lily and Joaquin will be pilots once they graduate from flight school.

10. During dinner, my Uncle Khalil had to go to the airport.

11. The clown would perform the trick, if only the rabbit was here.

12. After the aliens departed, the humans missed them.

13. The flowers are blooming, which Arturo predicted on Tuesday.

14. We will be on time, provided the shuttle arrives soon.

15. Even if the coffee is cold, I will still drink it.

Sentence Types
NOTES

Simple and Compound Sentences
NOTES

Sentence Types
Simple or Compound

A. Directions: Read the following sentences. Write an **S** in the blank if the sentence is a <u>simple sentence</u>, write a **C** in the blank if it is a <u>compound sentence</u>. If it is compound, circle the coordinating conjunction.

Examples: ___ He didn't win, so he lost. → **C** He didn't win,(so)he lost.
___ The big ogre ate a snail. → **S** The big ogre ate a snail.

1. ____ The acrobat came to my party, and the clown was jealous.

2. ____ Our dog is pregnant, so we will have puppies soon.

3. ____ Mabel and her brother drove a golf cart through the woods.

4. ____ Will the baboons and the orangutans enjoy this fruit basket?

5. ____ Her backpack got wet, yet her books stayed dry.

6. ____ Dr. Khan and Mr. Gates spoke at the last conference.

7. ____ The students brought pencils, erasers, and snacks for test day.

8. ____ Did you go to the store, or are we still out of milk?

9. ____ After the last announcement, the emcee dismissed the crowd.

10. ____ Turn off the lights, for it is time for bed.

11. ____ Would you like the cake, the pie, or the new cherry cheesecake.

12. ____ My parents are going to Hawaii, Florida, or the Carolinas in May.

13. ____ I wrote all night, but my novel is not finished.

14. ____ Nan and Ty ate and slept, and they had lovely dreams.

15. ____ The coffee shop on the corner is excellent.

**Sentence Types
Simple or Compound**

A. Directions: Read the following sentences. Write an **S** in the blank if the sentence is a <u>simple sentence</u>, write a **C** in the blank if it is a <u>compound sentence</u>. If it is compound, circle the coordinating conjunction.

Examples: __ They ran and jumped. → **S** They ran and jumped.
__ I tried, and it paid off. → **C** I tried, (and) it paid off.

1. ____ Zack gave his sister a thimble and blue ribbon.

2. ____ I like that cat, but this dog is my favorite.

3. ____ The moon is full, so the werewolves are out tonight.

4. ____ She found an old hat, jacket, and some leather shoes.

5. ____ Ramy and Abel climbed the mountain and hopped the fence.

6. ____ Our party can begin, for the dishes are clean.

7. ____ Without a paddle, it is difficult to steer a canoe.

8. ____ We need to brush our teeth, so we can go to bed.

9. ____ Their rocket ship flew to Jupiter yesterday after the ceremony.

10. ____ They enjoyed bananas, blueberries, cherries, and pears at the fair.

11. ____ My mom doesn't eat butter, nor does she drink milk.

12. ____ In the morning, we will go to the grocery store and the bank.

13. ____ Zelma went to the farmer's market, and she bought some kale.

14. ____ Are we taking the bus, or should we ride our bikes?

15. ____ Reid, Lou, Raya, and Uncle Nile are going to the game.

21

Complex and Compound-Complex Sentences
NOTES

List of Common Subordinating Conjunctions

After	Even if	Provided	Whenever
Although	Even though	Rather	Where
As	If	Since	Whereas
As if	If only	So that	Where if
As long as	If then	Supposing	Wherever
As much as	Just as	Than	Whether
As soon as	Now	That	Which
As though	Now since	Though	While
Because	Now that	Unless	Who
Before	Now when	Until	Whoever
Even	Once	When	Why

Sentence Types
Complex Sentences

A. Directions: Read the following <u>complex sentences</u>. Underline the <u>independent clause</u> once and circle the <u>subordinating conjunction</u>.

Example: People buy less when prices go up. ➔

<u>People buy less</u> (when) prices go up.

1. <u>She returned the soup</u> (after) she found a fly in it.

2. (Because) I missed the bus, <u>I was late for school</u>.

3. <u>The girl was happy to get a part in the play</u> (even though) it was small.

4. (Now that) her project is finished, <u>Naomi is going to the pool</u>.

5. <u>The rocket will not make it to the moon</u> (unless) we get fuel.

6. <u>That Chihuahua acts tough</u>, (as if) it was a big dog.

7. (Since) summer is coming, <u>Mom and Dad should buy a camper</u>.

8. <u>The boats will depart</u> (when) the tide rises.

9. <u>My typewriter is still broken</u> (even though) I tried to fix it.

10. (Although) it's 9am, <u>the sun is not in the sky in the Arctic Circle</u>.

11. <u>You can get a good grade</u> (as long as) you study regularly.

12. <u>The rain will fall</u> (whether) you want it to or not.

13. <u>Mr. Kurosaki was a poor man</u> (until) he became an inventor.

14. <u>I am tired, but they are staying here</u> (since) it's early.

15. (If) you drive the jetski, <u>we can get there faster</u>.

Sentence Types
Complex Sentences

A. Directions: Read the following sentences. Write a **C** in the blank if it is a complex sentence, and leave it blank if it is not. If it is a complex sentence, circle the subordinating conjunction.

Example: ___ Although he was rich, he was unhappy. →
C (Although) he was rich, he was unhappy.

1. ____ After the monsoon hit, the desert smelled wonderful.

2. ____ The museum was very interesting and not expensive.

3. ____ Wherever you go, you can always find beauty.

4. ____ The movie was excellent, as I expected.

5. ____ When did you fly on an airplane?

6. ____ My friends and I enjoyed the concert even though we were tired.

7. ____ I'll pay you back when the treasure is found.

8. ____ Their radio is on the windowsill so that they can hear it better.

9. ____ Did you celebrate now that you won the lottery?

10. ____ The chef is in the kitchen, and the hall is decorated.

11. ____ Ms. Nawaz went to the park and fed the ducks.

12. ____ We can clean up once the party is finished.

13. ____ You can play your video games as soon as your room is clean.

14. ____ If we go to school today, we won't have to go tomorrow.

15. ____ Rob drives carefully, but he's in a hurry since it is late.

Sentence Types
Compound-Complex Sentences

A. Directions: Read the following <u>compound-complex sentences</u>. Draw a circle the <u>coordinating conjunction</u>, and draw a rectangle around the <u>subordinating conjunction</u>.

    Example: He likes to sleep in, but he gets up early if he has to work.
   →   He likes to sleep in,(but)he gets up early [if] he has to work.

1. When I grow up, I want to be a doctor so I can help people.

2. They didn't win the game, yet they had fun which is what matters.

3. After his trip to California, school started, and he was excited to see friends.

4. Gabriela cried when her grandma got sick, but she got better quickly.

5. I was sleeping, and my daughter woke me up because she had a nightmare.

6. Ernie kept running, so he won the race then he collapsed.

7. When I was a child I was attacked by a dog, but I'm not afraid of them.

8. Rocko cried when I hit him with the ball, for he thought it was intentional.

9. She would have purchased the cookies that you like, but they were out of them at the store.

10. The sun finally came out, so I think that we can go to the pool.

Sentence Types
All Types

A. Directions: Read the following sentences. Write an **S** if the sentence is simple, **CP** if the sentence is compound, **CX** if it is complex, and **CPCX** if it is compound-complex.

1. _____ Out math books are heavy, so we carry them in backpacks.

2. _____ If you go out in the rain, you can't come back inside.

3. _____ The cow in the top hat went to the party on Saturday.

4. _____ I would have answered the phone when you called, but I was in the shower.

5. _____ Bigfoot went to the movies, but they would not sell him a ticket without a car.

6. _____ When it starts, the lights will dim, and the music will be loud.

7. _____ We need to get vaccinations before we travel to some countries.

8. _____ During the last parade, the biggest float got stuck in the underpass near Main Street.

9. _____ The bird healed because it rested, and it flew away.

10. _____ That ketchup stain remained even though I washed them twice.

11. _____ Those pirates want to buy new cell phones, laptops, and cars.

12. _____ The unicorns were endangered, for the faeries stole their magic.

Sentence Types (2)
NOTES

Sentence Types
Declarative, Imperative, Interrogative, & Exclamatory

A. Directions: In the blank, write the <u>sentence type</u> of the given sentence: **declarative**, **imperative**, **interrogative**, or **exclamatory**.

Example: _____ The guitar is red. ➔ _declarative_ The guitar is red.

1. _____ Do you have a question?

2. _____ There's a shark right there!

3. _____ Clean your room.

4. _____ Has the dog eaten dinner?

5. _____ My new bike is purple.

6. _____ Does their cat drink milk for breakfast?

7. _____ The house is on fire!

8. _____ Can you park your spaceship on asteroids?

9. _____ After the game, we are going to eat pizza.

10. _____ Follow the directions on the test.

11. _____ Tell me the truth about the kitchen.

12. _____ Malina's violin needs new strings.

13. _____ That unicorn snores in its sleep.

14. _____ I love eating tacos!

15. _____ Write an essay about your favorite cheese.

Sentence Types
Declarative, Imperative, Interrogative, & Exclamatory

A. Directions: In the blank, write the sentence type of the given sentence: **declarative**, **imperative**, **interrogative**, or **exclamatory**.

Example: _____ The guitar is red. → _declarative_ The guitar is red.

1. _____ Do you have a question?
2. _____ There's a shark right there!
3. _____ Clean your room.
4. _____ Has the dog eaten dinner?
5. _____ My new bike is purple.
6. _____ Does their cat drink milk for breakfast?

B. Directions: In the blanks, write a complete sentence for each type: **declarative**, **imperative**, **interrogative**, or **exclamatory**.

Declarative: _____
_____

Imperative: _____
_____

Interrogative: _____
_____

Exclamatory: _____
_____

List of Common Prepositions

A
About
Above
Across
After
Against
Along
Amid
Among
Around
At
Atop

B
Before
Behind
Below
Beneath
Beside
Between
Beyond
But (except)

C
Concerning

D
Down
During

E
Except

F
For
From

G

H

I
In
Inside
Into

J

K

L
Like

M

N
Near

O
Of
Off
On
Onto
Out
Outside
Over

P
Past

Q

R
Regarding

S
Since

T
Through
Throughout
To
Toward

U
Under
Underneath
Until
Up
Upon

V

W
With
Within
Without

X, Y, Z

Prepositions
NOTES

**Prepositions
NOTES**

Prepositions and Prepositional Phrases

A. Directions: Write a <u>preposition</u> in each blank to create a <u>prepositional phrase</u>. Use a different preposition in each blank.

Example: _____ the car ➔ <u>inside</u> the car **OR** <u>near</u> the car

1. _____ the fence
2. _____ a building
3. _____ his car
4. _____ 2pm
5. _____ lunch

6. _____ our banjo
7. _____ the moon
8. _____ my dinosaur
9. _____ two bikes
10. _____ an elephant

B. Directions: Write a preposition in each blank to create a prepositional phrase. Use a different preposition in each blank.

Example: _____ a pen ➔ <u>with</u> a pen **OR** <u>under</u> a pen

1. _____ his new coat
2. _____ a dishwasher
3. _____ school
4. _____ the taco shop
5. _____ those sharks

6. _____ her apartment
7. _____ three cats
8. _____ a library
9. _____ our friends
10. _____ worlds

**Prepositions and
Prepositional Phrases**

Directions: Write a sentence with the given <u>prepositional phrase</u>.

Example: into the maze → We will go ***into the maze*** tomorrow.
OR I went ***into the maze*** and got lost.

1. across the universe →

2. toward the monkey cage →

3. through the portal →

4. under the bridge →

5. over the unicorn →

6. at midnight →

7. on Tuesday →

8. of my computer →

9. with Mr. Morales →

10. during math class →

**Prepositions and
Prepositional Phrases**

Directions: Write a sentence with the given <u>prepositional phrase</u>.

Example: over the moon → The cow jumped **over the moon**.
OR **Over the moon**, I can see Mars.

1. beneath the clouds →
_____

2. onto the green sofa →
_____

3. after our first dinner →
_____

4. between those two trees →
_____

5. regarding your homework →
_____

6. in three months →
_____

7. on the clock tower →
_____

8. without my socks →
_____

9. except our kitten →
_____

10. throughout February and March →
_____

Prepositions and Prepositional Phrases

Directions: Draw a single line through <u>prepositional phrases</u>.
Underline the <u>simple subjects</u> once. Underline <u>verbs</u> twice.

Example: The brown cow jumped over the moon ➔
The brown <u>cow</u> <u>jumped</u> ~~over the moon~~.

1. Their pet mouse climbs into the cheese.

2. Dr. Phillips goes to his office.

3. A worm in your hand wriggles.

4. During recess, I read mythology books.

5. The woman beneath the car is a mechanic.

6. Our circus has shows on Sundays.

7. We sang many songs around the campfire.

8. The old robot across the street works slowly.

9. The family slept under the stars in their sleeping bags.

10. A man with a bowtie sells popcorn at the fair.

11. After work, my dad goes to the rec center.

12. Two baseball teams played a game of soccer.

13. His new puppy sleeps between two trees.

14. Ahmed goes to archery practice at 2pm.

15. Concerning math class, the girl in blue is the best.

Prepositions and Prepositional Phrases

Directions: Draw a single line through prepositional phrases. Underline the simple subjects once. Underline verbs twice.

Example: Bob Bobertson goes to the movies tomorrow. ➔
Bob Bobertson goes ~~to the movies~~ tomorrow.

1. The young king in the castle is lazy.
2. Ms. Garcia swims in the lap pool every day.
3. Our new camel sleeps in the house with us.
4. Three skunks with glasses read books about cheese.
5. I am scared of snakes in the grass.
6. Throughout the days, we sailed beyond the horizon.
7. The blanket sat atop the dryer underneath the jacket.
8. The kid against the wall rides bikes in the desert.
9. Flowers in vases are good gifts for anyone.
10. An elephant drove his new car around the corner.
11. The state senators in our state have meetings until dinner.
12. Everyone except Octavia went into the fun house.
13. He went past his exit during the storm.
14. My spaceship sits upon a moon around Jupiter.
15. That octopus with the drumsticks plays in the band.

Prepositions and Prepositional Phrases

Directions: Draw a single line through <u>prepositional phrases</u>. Underline the <u>simple subjects</u> once. Underline <u>verbs</u> twice.

Example: Twelve red dinosaurs with goggles swam across the lake. ➔
Twelve red <u>dinosaurs</u> ~~with goggles~~ <u><u>swam</u></u> ~~across the lake~~.

1. A long <u>tunnel</u> <u><u>runs</u></u> ~~through the mountain~~.

2. The <u>cat</u> ~~in boots~~ <u><u>has</u></u> a hat ~~with a feather~~.

3. Ten <u>drums</u> <u><u>are</u></u> ~~in the office~~ ~~behind the band room~~.

4. ~~In the morning~~, Dr. <u>Ejogo</u> <u><u>swims</u></u> ~~in the ocean~~.

5. Your <u>dragon</u> <u><u>flies</u></u> ~~around the second blue moon~~.

6. <u>Coyotes</u> ~~of the desert~~ <u><u>are</u></u> survivors.

7. The famous <u>artist</u> <u><u>paints</u></u> ~~on the walls~~ ~~of buildings~~.

8. ~~Outside the city~~, a <u>farmer</u> <u><u>raises</u></u> alpacas ~~for fun~~.

9. My <u>socks</u> ~~underneath the bed~~ <u><u>are filled</u></u> ~~with holes~~.

10. The <u>lawyer</u> <u><u>explained</u></u> matters ~~concerning our case~~.

11. Ray's <u>computer</u> <u><u>remains</u></u> ~~at the shop~~ ~~until tomorrow~~.

12. Five red <u>foxes</u> <u><u>frolic</u></u> ~~across the forest floor~~.

13. All <u>students</u> ~~but one~~ <u><u>voted</u></u> ~~for Nihal~~ ~~in the election~~.

14. ~~Within the submarine~~, a <u>sailor</u> <u><u>wrote</u></u> letters ~~to his kids~~.

15. A <u>mouse</u> <u><u>ran</u></u> ~~into the kitchen~~, ~~onto the counter~~, and ~~toward the cheese~~.

**Compounds
Subjects or Verbs**

Directions: Underline the simple <u>compound subjects</u> once, <u>verbs</u> twice, and cross out any <u>prepositional phrases</u>.

　　Example: Dogs and cats sit on mats. ➔ <u>Dogs</u> and <u>cats</u> <u>sit</u> ~~on mats~~.

1. Kwame and Sue go to the same school.

2. The horse and the cow live in the barn.

3. In the afternoon, she and the doctor play chess.

4. The dog with spots and our cat sleep quietly.

5. A dragon and an ogre have tea in the castle.

6. Irma Gerd and her iguana drive through the country.

Directions: Underline the <u>simple subjects</u> once, <u>compound verbs</u> twice, and cross out any <u>prepositional phrases</u>.

　　Example: She runs and jumps over it. ➔ <u>She</u> <u>runs</u> and <u>jumps</u> ~~over it~~.

1. Those students swim and dive for the school.

2. A bowling ball is heavy and has three holes.

3. Jon Yonson likes cheese and makes cheddar at home.

4. At the game, the player kicked the ball hard and ran.

5. Our flowers grow tall and make seeds for the future.

6. The caterpillar crawls across the leaf and rests.

**Compounds
Subjects or Verbs**

Directions: Underline the simple compound subjects once, verbs twice, and cross out any prepositional phrases.

Example: After tea, Ryo and Lee nap. ➔ ~~After tea~~, Ryo and Lee nap.

1. The surfboard and skateboard are in the garage.

2. Naomi Kwan and Dr. Philips climb up the mountain.

3. During the snowstorm, my mom and I saved a dog.

4. The cow in the meadow and that goat have a business.

5. A shiny new penny and an old quarter sit on the table.

6. Their house and office exist on the same street.

Directions: Underline the simple subjects once, compound verbs twice, and cross out any prepositional phrases.

Example: We go to stores and shop. ➔ We go ~~to stores~~ and shop.

1. Vlad walks to school and drives to his office.

2. My old jacket has holes and needs patches on the elbows.

3. Under the ocean, weird fish swim and hunt in darkness.

4. Her boots with zippers feel comfortable and smell bad.

5. Our cat sleeps in the day and eats at night.

6. Homer has a long beard and writes with a quill.

Compounds
Objects of the Prepositions

Directions: Underline the simple subjects once, the verbs twice, and cross out prepositional phrases with compound objects of the preposition.

   Example: I swim in lakes and rivers. ➔ I swim in lakes and rivers.

1. That squirrel with the suit and brief case hires lawyers.

2. The twins went to the arcade or the movies.

3. Between lunch and dinner, we have tea.

4. Our friends run through fields and meadows.

5. Lakshmi cooks with chefs or sous-chefs.

6. The mighty saguaro grows near the mesquite and creosote.

7. Mr. Jansen, in the suit and tie, sells used cars.

8. We traveled across galaxies and solar systems.

9. Among cows, goats, and horses, they collect flowers.

10. The land of milk and honey seems far.

11. Her new rabbit sleeps under sheets and blankets.

12. Two llamas wrote a book regarding grass and hay.

13. We leave on Monday, Tuesday, or Thursday.

14. Everyone except Kamala and Benny surf today.

15. They wrote a book about rockets, slime, butterflies, candy, or tadpoles.

**Compounds
Review**

Directions: Underline any <u>simple subjects</u> once, underline all <u>verbs</u> twice, and cross out any prepositional phrases.

Example: We eat and drink with friends. →
<u>We</u> <u>eat</u> and <u>drink</u> ~~with friends.~~

1. Pancho and Lefty ride their horses to a small Mexican town.

2. The beautiful red deer jumped over the fence and ran.

3. Those professors with the wild hair and glasses teach physics.

4. Our grandma and uncle drove to the store and bought gifts.

5. Mr. Afumba and his niece ride motorbikes in the afternoon.

6. Piper, Bilal, and their dog eat peanut butter from the jar.

7. An antelope sprints through the mall and the food court.

8. Tia Valeria writes, designs, and publishes books in New York.

9. My dad will fly to Chicago, Shanghai, Sao Paolo, or Oslo.

10. After their last class and practice, they go to the library.

11. Faheem and the ancient wizard shared ice cream in August.

12. I went to the movies with Isla, Ayaka, Paula, Dorian, Leon, and Bexley.

13. My puppy and your kitten play and nap in the backyard.

14. Rabia, her sister, and a friend watched movies in the den.

15. Clowns, acrobats, and jugglers work and play in big tents and arenas.

Nouns
NOTES

Nouns
Common and Proper

A. Directions: In the blank, write if the given noun is <u>common</u> or <u>proper</u>.

Examples: _____ CAT ➔ <u>common</u> CAT
_____ UTAH ➔ <u>proper</u> UTAH

1. _____ BIKE
2. _____ ZEBRA
3. _____ SEATTLE
4. _____ GLASSES
5. _____ ROBERT

6. _____ CALENDAR
7. _____ TEXAS
8. _____ FRANCE
9. _____ UMBRELLA
10. _____ ENGLISH

B. Directions: In the blank, write a <u>proper noun</u> example for each <u>common noun</u> given.

Examples: _____ country ➔ <u>Canada</u> country
_____ human ➔ <u>Tina</u> human

1. _____ city
2. _____ state
3. _____ river
4. _____ actor
5. _____ scientist

6. _____ school
7. _____ college
8. _____ ocean
9. _____ mountain
10. _____ building

Nouns
Common and Proper

A. Directions: Circle all the common nouns. When you're done, count them and write the total number here: _____

DOG   PIZZA   MEXICO   TESLA   BOOK   PARIS   OCTOPUS

HEART   JAPAN   DRAGON   FRIDAY   ATLANTIC   TRUMPET

PILLOW   SHOES   CLAUDIA   GIRAFFE   EINSTEIN   NILE

GERMAN   ROBINSON   DAY   WATCH   DORITOS   TRUCK

OCTOBER   BOSTON   MARIO   TEETH   APARTMENT   ANNA

BOOTS   COCA-COLA   ROBLOX   AFRICA   SNAKE   CANDLE

B. Directions: Circle all the proper nouns. When you're done, count them and write the total number here: _____

RADIO   TABLE   NINTENDO   TOOTHBRUSH   NAVAJO   TAP

PUG   MONSTER   MEDITTERANIAN   IRAN   BRICK   JACKET

SAN DIEGO   MONDAY   FLOWER   GRAVEYARD   TOKYO   KNIFE

RUSSIAN   EAGLE   SUNGLASSES   HANNAH   IOWA

INDIA   TITANIC   MISSISSIPPI   THOMAS   CALF   LONDON

CLEOPATRA   PINEAPPLE   SHIRT   NIGERIA   CREEK   ROD

**Nouns
Concrete and Abstract**

Directions: In the blank, write if the given noun is concrete or abstract.

Examples: _____ drum ➔ _concrete_ drum
_____ joy ➔ _proper_ joy

1. _____ truck
2. _____ freedom
3. _____ glasses
4. _____ mailman
5. _____ justice
6. _____ feathers
7. _____ peace
8. _____ kindness
9. _____ robe
10. _____ city
11. _____ patience
12. _____ fedora
13. _____ ladder
14. _____ warmth
15. _____ happiness
16. _____ chaos
17. _____ truth
18. _____ pilot
19. _____ sword
20. _____ democracy
21. _____ river
22. _____ ocean
23. _____ wealth
24. _____ bookshelf
25. _____ sadness
26. _____ opinion
27. _____ parent
28. _____ parenthood
29. _____ violins
30. _____ thought

Nouns
Concrete and Abstract

Directions: Write sentences using the <u>abstract nouns</u> provided.

   Example: IDEA: ➔   I have an IDEA.
                     OR   The IDEA is good.

1. INFORMATION: _____

_____

2. ENERGY: _____

_____

3. FRIENDSHIP: _____

_____

4. ANGER: _____

_____

5. WISDOM: _____

_____

6. FAILURE: _____

_____

7. LOYALTY: _____

_____

8. BEAUTY: _____

_____

Nouns
Subjects and Objects

A. Directions: Each of the following sentences is missing a <u>subject</u>. Write a noun into the blank to complete the sentence.

Example: The _____ goes to school. ➔ The <u>kid</u> goes to school.

1. Ten silly _____ gallop toward the ocean.

2. Our antique _____ is in the shop for repairs.

3. Ji-yoo and Viggo's _____ takes naps in the afternoon.

4. _____ paints enormous murals on the school.

5. The _____ and a _____ go to the moon.

B. Directions: Each of the following sentences is missing an <u>object of the preposition</u> or a <u>direct object</u>. Write a noun into the blank to complete the sentence.

Example: Nancy swims with _____. ➔ Nancy swims with <u>sharks</u>.

1. After _____, we will pilot our spaceship to Jupiter.

2. The strong girl lifted the _____ in the junkyard.

3. A fast mouse escaped between a _____ and a _____.

4. Abdallah and his friends carved _____ into the log.

5. The man with seven _____ has super-powers.

Nouns
Pronouns (intro)

A. Directions: Write the correct <u>subject pronoun</u> (I, you, he, she, it, we, they) into the blank to complete the sentence.

    Example: (Bob and Jess) _____ go to work. ➔
                      <u> They </u> go to work.

1. (You and I) _____ write our names in ink.

2. (My Aunt Maude) _____ is a banker in Seattle.

3. (a barn) _____ has no paint on the walls.

4. (*you*) _____ am an excellent student.

5. (Uma, Chuck, and Isak) _____ have the same hat.

B. Directions: Write the correct <u>object pronoun</u> (me, you, him, her, it, us, them) into the blank to complete the sentence.

    Example: (You and I) The dogs swim with _____. ➔
                    The dogs swim with <u> us </u>.

1. (people) Savannah waited in line with _____.

2. (Grandpa) The cheetah ran toward _____ yesterday.

3. (*a person you're talking to*) I told _____ a long story.

4. (Santino and Esme) The driver took _____ to the airport.

5. (a wall) The girl threw the ball against _____.

Adjectives
NOTES

Adjectives
Descriptive Adjectives

Directions: Write 3 adjectives to describe each noun.

    Example: Dog
                         _____playful_____
                         _____loyal_____
                         _____kind_____

1. Bicycle

_____
_____
_____

2. Dinosaur

_____
_____
_____

3. Suitcase

_____
_____
_____

4. Television

_____
_____
_____

5. Piano

_____
_____
_____

6. Scissors

_____
_____
_____

7. Lawn

_____
_____
_____

8. Cactus

_____
_____
_____

Adjectives
Descriptive Adjectives

A. Directions: Write <u>descriptive adjectives</u> into the blanks to complete the prepositional phrases.

1. near a _____ tree
2. into _____ stores
3. under _____ clothes
4. during _____ holidays
5. for the _____ birds
6. atop _____ tent
7. except _____ grandmas
8. off his _____ head
9. until an _____ day
10. from _____ students

11. across the _____ road
12. with a _____ donkey
13. down the _____ slide
14. over _____ mountains
15. to our _____ house
16. among _____ penguins
17. toward their _____ boat
18. onto a _____ truck
19. without her _____ bag
20. amid many _____ boxes

B. Directions: Write a <u>descriptive adjective</u> in each blank to complete the sentences of the paragraph.

One day, the _____ dragon flew to a _____ swamp. He met two _____ and _____ gnomes. They needed help getting _____ fruits from a very _____ tree. After the dragon helped, the gnomes were so _____ that they gave it a _____ and _____ treasure.

Adjectives
Descriptive Adjectives

Directions: Write <u>descriptive adjectives</u> into the blanks that start with each letter of the alphabet.

1. **A**_____
2. **B**_____
3. **C**_____
4. **D**_____
5. **E**_____
6. **F**_____
7. **G**_____
8. **H**_____
9. **I**_____
10. **J**_____
11. **K**_____
12. **L**_____
13. **M**_____
14. **N**_____
15. **O**_____

16. **P**_____
17. **Q**_____
18. **R**_____
19. **S**_____
20. **T**_____
21. **U**_____
22. **V**_____
23. **W**_____
24. **X**_____
25. **Y**_____
26. **Z**_____

Adjectives
Descriptive Adjectives

Directions: Circle all of the <u>descriptive adjectives</u> in the following sentences.

1. The quirky rabbit jumped over the lazy toad.

2. After the terrible race, my great friend gave me a big hug.

3. Her new bike has red and blue stripes on the shiny metal.

4. Did the sweet grandma tell the funny story about cute sloths?

5. A large basket with fuzzy kittens sat on the nice porch.

6. Her backpack is new, blue, sturdy, and fantastic!

7. That tiny mouse hides between the broken teacups.

8. I like the scruffy donkey with the big ugly sweater.

9. An aggressive goose attacked the happy picnic.

10. Go to the huge market and buy some fresh fruits and vegetables.

11. Without reliable seatbelts, cars are dangerous.

12. The best classroom has large windows and beautiful decorations.

13. A friendly dragon performed a spectacular dance at the fun party.

14. That small and remote town has delicious ice cream.

15. At my cool school, the young math teacher wears strange glasses.

Limiting Adjectives
NOTES

**Limiting Adjectives/
Noun Determiners**

A. Directions: Circle all of the <u>articles</u> (a, an, the). Draw an arrow to the noun that they point to.

Example: The cat climbs a tree. → (The)↷cat climbs a tree.

1. An aardvark and a porcupine go to the movies.

2. The tide comes in on the beach in an hour.

3. During a break, the players ate an orange.

B. Directions: Circle all of the <u>demonstratives</u> (this, that, these, those). Draw an arrow to the noun that they point to.

1. Will those toys fit into this cardboard box?

2. These motorcycles go onto that truck this morning.

3. Take that water bottle and these vitamins to the second floor.

4. On Tuesday, she will drive this truck through those mountains.

C. Directions: Circle all of the <u>numbers</u>. Draw an arrow to the noun that they point to.

1. One cat escaped the crate with four toys.

2. After 17 hours, the team scored two points.

3. Twenty-two monkeys ate seventy bananas with two gorillas.

4. Can eight friends share two bedrooms?

**Limiting Adjectives/
Noun Determiners**

A. Directions: Circle all of the possessive nouns (Ex: Bob's). Draw an arrow to the noun that they point to.

Example: The dog's bowl is empty. ➔ The (dog's) bowl is empty.

1. Bella's horse is faster than Yuri's reindeer.

2. A dinosaur's claw is in the museum's exhibit.

3. During Mr. Cooper's class, my pencil's eraser broke.

B. Directions: Circle all of the possessive pronouns (Ex: her, their). Draw an arrow to the noun that they point to.

1. My wallet is in her backpack at his house.

2. On their birthday, the twins had a party at our house.

3. Your globe is in their classroom on its stand.

4. Whose present is a ride in our new rocket?

C. Directions: Circle all of the indefinites (Ex: few, some). Draw an arrow to the noun that they point to.

1. Some students forget to study any notes.

2. In many months, few inches of rain fell in town.

3. I gave several treats to most dogs at the park.

4. There are no fish in most canals and some rivers.

Limiting Adjectives/
Noun Determiners

Directions: Write the requested <u>limiting adjective/noun determiner</u> into each blank to complete the sentences, then draw an arrow to the noun it modifies.

Examples: (Article) _____ tank is full. → <u>The</u> tank is full.

(Indefinite) I have ____ cars. → I have <u>few</u> cars.

1. (Article) – We buy _____ donuts on Sundays.

2. (Demonstrative) – _____ bowl of cereal is your breakfast.

3. (Number) – That clown has _____ multi-colored balloons.

4. (Possessive Pronoun) – George drives _____ new car.

5. (Possessive Noun) – The _____ banana is green.

6. (Indefinite) – Scientists sat at a picnic table with _____ friends.

7. (Article) – Can we take _____ airplane to Canada?

8. (Demonstrative) – _____ submarine travels quickly.

9. (Number) – Our _____ poodles are all sick.

10. (Possessive Pronoun) – Grandma Jane made _____ sweaters.

11. (Possessive Noun) – I broke _____ coffee mug.

12. (Indefinite) – _____ parties are not very fun.

13. (Your choice) – Tam did homework with _____ pencils.

**Limiting Adjectives/
Noun Determiners**

Directions: Circle all of the <u>limiting adjectives/noun determiners</u>. Draw an arrow to the noun that they point to.

Example: The dog's bowl is empty. →

1. The piano sits in Diane's living room.

2. Four monkeys played in that orchestra.

3. Mrs. Wiggins has a unicorn with some fancy clothes.

4. Their flag flies on that flagpole in the summertime.

5. Alexandra's mittens have three holes.

6. An aardvark snoops for many ants.

7. We have no chocolate and ten lollipops.

8. Those cyclists are in our way.

9. Whose ghosts haunted this school?

10. Several toys fell behind a dresser in the playroom.

11. Does that girl have any horses?

12. Take these pencils to Mr. Lee's classroom.

13. Aaliyah's cousin takes his math test on a computer.

14. After our game, we went to her pizza parlor.

15. The ten kangaroos drove into that forest.

Limiting Adjectives/ Noun Determiners

Directions: The words in *italics* are on the limiting adjectives/noun determiners list. Write an <u>A</u> in the blank if they are behaving like an *adjective*. Write a <u>P</u> in the blank if they are behaving like a *pronoun*. If it is behaving like an *adjective*, draw an arrow from it to the noun it's modifying.

Examples: ___ *This* cup is empty. → _A_ *This* cup is empty.

___ I like *this*. → _P_ I like *this*.

1. _____ *Both* will go to the horse race.

2. _____ They like *those* bracelets with the jewels.

3. _____ Sheila will take *ten*.

4. _____ *That* man has a sword from ancient Japan.

5. _____ I believe that *this* is mine.

6. _____ Put more pepper on *that*, please.

7. _____ We have *few* hot dogs in stock.

8. _____ There are *six* dinosaurs in the museum.

9. _____ *Many* of the babies are hungry.

10. _____ The big box store will have *several* on the shelf.

11. _____ Are there *any* tickets for the show?

12. _____ Molly wants *some* of the peaches.

Limiting Adjectives/
Noun Determiners

Directions: The words in *italics* are on the limiting adjectives/noun determiners list. Write an A in the blank if they are behaving like an *adjective*. Write a P in the blank if they are behaving like a *pronoun*. If it is behaving like an *adjective*, draw an arrow from it to the noun it's modifying.

Examples: ___ *Many* have tried.   →   _P_ *Many* have tried.

___ I have *many* hats.   →   _A_ I have *many* hats.

1. _____ *Some* gophers read in the dark.

2. _____ *Few* of the students failed the last test.

3. _____ We have *many* in the pantry.

4. _____ Morris took *those* to the dry cleaners.

5. _____ We have *this* book in our English class.

6. _____ Will you go with *her*?

7. _____ Will you go with *her* mother?

8. _____ *Four* senators ate all the chicken patties.

9. _____ The very hungry dogs ate *ten*.

10. _____ *Those* are mine!

11. _____ *Whose* backpack is on the car?

12. _____ *Many* of the dragons have bad teeth.

Predicate Adjective
NOTES

Adjectives
Predicate Adjectives

A. Directions: Draw a line between the complete subject and the complete predicate. Circle the predicate adjective.

Examples: Her snake with stripes was hungry. →

Her snake with stripes | was (hungry)

1. The beautiful lizard looks warm on that rock.

2. A robot with a bowtie is cool.

3. After school, my mom was happy.

4. Mr. Zelinsky was nervous about his driving test.

5. Our big brown horse is lazy in the afternoon.

B. Directions: Draw a line through any prepositional phrases. Underline the simple subject once, the verbs twice. Circle the predicate adjective.

Examples: Her snake with stripes is hungry. →

Her <u>snake</u> ~~with stripes~~ <u><u>was</u></u> (hungry)

1. The beautiful lizard looks warm on that rock.

2. A robot with a bowtie is cool.

3. After school, my mom was happy.

4. Mr. Zelinsky was nervous about his driving test.

5. Our big brown horse is lazy in the afternoon.

Adjectives
Predicate Adjectives

A. Directions: Draw a line between the <u>complete subject</u> and the <u>complete predicate</u>. Circle the <u>predicate adjective</u>.

Examples: The sun is warm by ten.   ➔   The sun | is (warm) by ten.

1. Your garden appears green in the morning light.

2. Mr. Gomez and Ms. Jenkins are angry regarding the fight.

3. Between two trees, the deer seems peaceful.

4. A gorilla among the monkeys is tall.

5. The mountains with cabins were cold during winter.

B. Directions: Draw a line through any <u>prepositional phrases</u>. Underline the <u>simple subject</u> once, the <u>verbs</u> twice. Circle the <u>predicate adjective</u>.

Examples: The sun is warm by ten.   ➔   The <u>sun</u> <u>is</u> (warm) by ten.

1. Your garden appears green in the morning light.

2. Mr. Gomez and Ms. Jenkins are angry regarding the fight.

3. Between two trees, the deer seems peaceful.

4. A gorilla among the monkeys is tall.

5. The mountains with cabins were cold during winter.

Adjectives
Predicate Adjectives

Directions: Draw a line through any <u>prepositional phrases</u>. Underline the <u>simple subject</u> once, the <u>verbs</u> twice. Circle the <u>predicate adjective</u>.

Examples: In an hour, we will be thirsty. →

~~In an hour~~, <u>we</u> <u><u>will be</u></u> (thirsty)

1. Dr. Bhat was sleepy after work.

2. The new dishwasher in the kitchen is excellent.

3. An old man looks fancy with a tuxedo.

4. During swim practice, I became tired.

5. His new jacket on the floor is dirty.

6. That magical mirror on the wall was broken.

7. In three days, we will be relaxed at the spa.

8. The dragon at the pool is scared of water.

9. Her video game concerning aliens is fun.

10. A man with glasses seems intelligent.

11. Ms. Byers looks joyful between the palm trees.

12. In the barn, the cows are confused.

13. Chris and Kamal were lucky in the last race.

14. Our bandages were perfect for our costume.

15. After the ride, their sunglasses seemed dirty.

Adjectives
Predicate Adjectives

Directions: Draw a line through any prepositional phrases. Underline the simple subject once, the verbs twice. Circle the predicate adjective.

Examples: The girl was tired in the morning. →

The girl was (tired) ~~in the morning~~.

1. A team of oxen at the farm is strong.

2. Khalil and Tara were happy after the circus.

3. The comedian from that show was funny.

4. Before sunset, the sun seems bigger.

5. Those muffins in the oven smell sweet and delicious.

6. Our two cats will be angry after our vacation.

7. The sunglasses on her head were shiny.

8. Dad and his sister are nervous during family reunions.

9. My face feels sticky on very hot days.

10. Uncle Diego's new suit is blue like the sky.

11. Without a hat, a head becomes cold in the winter.

12. Her pearls were expensive for a birthday present.

13. The phone on the counter is broken and old.

14. Swimsuits, towels, and sunscreen are necessary at the beach.

15. This bank vault in the basement is strong and appears secure.

Verb Tenses
NOTES

Verb Tenses
Past, Present, and Future

Directions: Write the past, present and future tenses for each of the infinitive verbs given.

Example: **TO JUMP**
past: _____jumped_____
present: _____jump(s)_____
future: _____will jump_____

1. **TO PLAY**

    past:_____

    present:_____

    future:_____

2. **TO SOAR**

    past:_____

    present:_____

    future:_____

3. **TO PERFORM**

    past:_____

    present:_____

    future:_____

4. **TO STAY**

    past:_____

    present:_____

    future:_____

5. **TO ARRIVE**

    past:_____

    present:_____

    future:_____

6. **TO WALK**

    past:_____

    present:_____

    future:_____

7. **TO SCRIBBLE**

    past:_____

    present:_____

    future:_____

8. **TO CLOSE**

    past:_____

    present:_____

    future:_____

Verb Tenses
Past, Present, and Future

A. Directions: In the blank, write the past tense form of the verb given to complete each sentence.

    Example: A frog (**to jump**) _____. ➔ A frog (**to jump**) _jumped_.

1. Yesterday, we (**to play**) _____ our instruments at school.

2. The androids (**to rescue**) _____ the crew last month.

3. Two years ago, I (**to lift**) _____ weights at the gym.

B. Directions: In the blank, write the present tense form of the verb given to complete each sentence.

    Example: The cheetah (**to run**) ____. ➔ The cheetah (**to run**) _runs_.

1. Today, they (**to swim**) _____ across the lake.

2. Our dog (**to walk**) _____ to the park every day.

3. Kamala and I (**to drive**) _____ our go-carts now.

C. Directions: In the blank, write the future tense form of the verb given to complete each sentence.

    Example: The rat (**to eat**) _____. ➔ The rat (**to eat**) _will eat_.

1. Tomorrow, an author (**to visit**) _____ our school.

2. In the future, I (**to be**) _____ a juggler in the circus.

3. They (**to say**) _____ goodbye after the concert.

Verb Tenses
Past, Present, and Future

A. Directions: In the blank, write any verb in its past tense form to complete each sentence.

   Example: A kid _____ a toy to me. ➔ A kid _tossed_ a toy to me.

1. Those funky dinosaurs _____ guitars in their sleep.

2. Darcy's platypus _____ on the grass.

3. A wildcat with glasses _____ the book.

B. Directions: In the blank, write any verb in its present tense form to complete each sentence.

   Example: Bob _____ to the store. ➔ Bob _scoots_ to the store.

1. The whole planet _____ around the sun.

2. Our old babysitter _____ for NASA now.

3. _____ your room before bed.

C. Directions: In the blank, write any verb in its future tense form to complete each sentence.

   Example: The car _____ soon. ➔ The car _will explode_ soon.

1. Later today, we _____ to the hair salon.

2. Some students _____ engineers in the future.

3. _____ you _____ to the movies?

Action Verbs / Linking Verbs
NOTES

Verbs
Action Verbs or Linking Verbs

A. Directions: In the blank, write an **A** if the verb is an <u>action verb</u>, leave it blank if it is not an action verb.

Examples: ____ to jump ➔ _A_ to jump

1. ____ to swim
2. ____ ran
3. ____ were
4. ____ to spin
5. ____ left

6. ____ is
7. ____ to climb
8. ____ drives
9. ____ attempted
10. ____ to be

11. ____ to play
12. ____ to cross
13. ____ flew
14. ____ are
15. ____ seemed

B. Directions: Draw a line through any <u>prepositional phrases</u>. Underline the <u>simple subject</u> once and the <u>verbs</u> twice. In the blank, write an **A** if the verb is an <u>action verb</u>, leave it blank if it is not an action verb.

Examples: ____ He runs on trails. ➔ _A_ He <u>runs</u> <s>on trails</s>.
 ____ She is kind with kids. ➔ ____ <u>She</u> <u>is</u> kind <s>with kids</s>.

1. ____ At night, the musician played his saxophone on the bridge.

2. ____ That young woman in blue was messy during cooking class.

3. ____ The pepperoni pizzas are frozen within the freezer.

4. ____ Mr. Spiller and his iguana from Ecuador climbed Mt. Kilimanjaro.

5. ____ Beyond the stars, a lonely planet seems lost in darkness.

Verbs
Action Verbs or Linking Verbs

A. Directions: In each blank, write an <u>action verb</u> in its <u>infinitive</u> form.

Examples: to run, to jump, to fly

1. _____   4. _____   7. _____

2. _____   5. _____   8. _____

3. _____   6. _____   9. _____

B. Directions: There are only <u>12</u> linking verbs, write them in their <u>infinitive</u> forms in the blanks below.

1. _____   5. _____   9. _____

2. _____   6. _____   10. _____

3. _____   7. _____   11. _____

4. _____   8. _____   12. _____

C. Directions: In the following sentences, underline the verbs twice. Write an **L** in the blank if it is behaving as a linking verb and an **A** if it is an action.

Examples: ____ He smells bad.   →   _L_ He <u>smells</u> bad.
            ____ He smells a rose.   →   _A_ He <u>smells</u> a rose.

1. ____ The mushroom soup tasted delicious.

2. ____ Our dog tastes his bone in the backyard.

3. ____ A blind person feels the walls in the hall.

4. ____ In the afternoon, my grandmother feels tired.

Verbs
Action Verbs or Linking Verbs

Directions: Draw a line through any prepositional phrases. Underline the simple subject once and verbs twice. If the verb is a <u>linking</u> verb, write an **L** in the blank. If it is an <u>action</u> verb, write an **A**.

Examples: ____ She feels the fruit. → __A__ She <u>feels</u> the fruit.
____ It feels hot in June. → __L__ It <u>feels</u> hot ~~in June~~.

1. ____ Her grill on the patio smells smoky.

2. ____ The magical sword seems shiny in the firelight.

3. ____ That cat on the windowsill looks at the goldfish.

4. ____ Grandma's basket appears full of apples.

5. ____ Ferdinand smells the daisies in the field.

6. ____ A turtle on a bicycle jumped over the canyon.

7. ____ Whose socks smell bad after practice?

8. ____ My new camera became useful at work.

9. ____ Darlene feels the window for scratches.

10. ____ Those jackets on the coatrack are warm.

11. ____ Snakes strike quickly in the desert.

12. ____ A scary old castle will feel comfortable.

13. ____ During breakfast, I tasted the scramble eggs.

14. ____ Our horses grow tired after a long trip in the country.

Verbs
Action Verbs or Linking Verbs

Directions: Draw a line through any prepositional phrases. Underline the simple subject once and verbs twice. If the verb is a <u>linking</u> verb, write an **L** in the blank. If it is an <u>action</u> verb, write an **A**.

Examples: ____ Dad tastes the soup. → __A__ Dad <u>tastes</u> the soup.
____ It tastes good in tea. → __L__ It <u>tastes</u> good in tea.

1. ____ The full moon appears large above the mountains.

2. ____ Mr. Robbins sang cowboy songs on a horse.

3. ____ During the celebration, the horse stayed calm.

4. ____ Their kite with yellow ribbons looks lovely in the blue sky.

5. ____ The security guard in the booth sounds the alarm.

6. ____ Your guitar on the wall sounds loud.

7. ____ A bloodhound smells a deer on the trail.

8. ____ Without cheese, this burrito tastes terrible.

9. ____ Uncle Carlos rode his motorcycle through the country.

10. ____ A bull became tranquil on the other side of the fence.

11. ____ The long-distance runner grows tired after 20 miles.

12. ____ Conan's audience looked at the comedian.

13. ____ That man's unicycle seems new since the rain.

14. ____ An unknown object appeared over New York City.

15. ____ Some small seeds become huge trees with time.

Linking Verbs / Predicate Adjectives / Predicate Nominatives
NOTES

Linking Verbs
Predicate Adjectives

Directions: Draw a line through any <u>prepositional phrases</u>. Underline the <u>simple subject</u> once and <u>verbs</u> twice. If the verb is a <u>linking verb</u>, does it link to a <u>predicate adjective</u>? If so, circle the predicate adjective.

    Examples: He smells the tea. ➔ He <u>smells</u> the tea.
                        It seems good to him. ➔ It <u>seems</u> (good) ~~to him~~.

1. The teachers are kind to the new students.

2. Mr. Liu tastes every cupcake at the bake sale.

3. Aunt Fran's chinchilla feels soft on my skin.

4. After dinner, we tried a dessert from Iran.

5. Those turtles in the pond smell funky.

6. Our new chair on the porch feels comfortable.

7. Their puppy smells everything from the store.

8. A new song on the radio sounded excellent.

9. In the workroom, the computer's screen is broken.

10. During the fall, the bears become sleepy.

11. An iceberg in the arctic is travelling north.

12. The cheese on the counter seems moldy.

13. A magical fairy appeared amidst the trees.

14. Milo's sword shines brightly in his hand.

15. My dog becomes tired after a long day.

Linking Verbs
Predicate Nominatives

A. Directions: Draw a line between the complete subject and the complete predicate. Circle the predicate nominative.

Examples: At camp, our parents were lifeguards. →

At camp, our parents | were (lifeguards)

1. Their new cameras were gifts from a kind stranger.

2. After the swim meet, I am the champion.

3. That dog with the bandana is a fast runner.

4. An ice cream sundae was our reward at the fair.

5. The candle and the soap are bribes for my mom.

B. Directions: Draw a line through any prepositional phrases. Underline the simple subject once, the verbs twice. Circle the predicate nominative.

Examples: At camp, our parents were lifeguards. →

~~At camp~~, our <u>parents</u> <u>were</u> (lifeguards)

1. Their new cameras were gifts from a kind stranger.

2. After the swim meet, I am the champion.

3. That dog with the bandana is a fast runner.

4. An ice cream sundae was our reward at the fair.

5. The candle and the soap are bribes for my mom.

Linking Verbs
Predicate Nominatives

A. Directions: Draw a line through any prepositional phrases. Underline the simple subject once and linking verbs twice. Circle the predicate nominatives.

Examples: The man in red is our teacher. →

The man ~~in red~~ is our (teacher)

1. That donkey with a sweater is my grandpa's best friend.

2. Our rags in the garage were t-shirts.

3. During the parade, his car was a colorful float.

4. Gael and Zara are the nicest students at school.

5. My mom will be a scientist and a doctor after graduation.

B. Directions: Underline the simple subject once and linking verbs twice. If the sentence has a predicate nominative, write **PN** in the blank. If it has a predicate adjective, write **PA**.

Examples: ____ His cat is soft. → **PA** His cat is soft.
____ A cat is his pet. → **PN** A cat is his pet.

1. ____ My new juggling clubs are my toys.

2. ____ The tuba was his instrument.

3. ____ Our house seems humongous.

4. ____ Those blackbirds are scavengers.

5. ____ Your motorcycle is a dangerous vehicle.

Linking Verbs
Predicate Nominatives and Adjectives

Directions: Draw a line through prepositional phrases. Underline the simple subject once and linking verbs twice. Circle any predicate adjectives or predicate nominatives. If the sentence has a predicate nominative, write **PN** in the blank. If it has a predicate adjective, write **PA**.

Examples: ___ A lady on TV is sad. → **PA** A lady on TV is sad.
___ Theo was a doctor. → **PN** Theo was a doctor.

1. _____ Their lawyers are the people on the stairs.

2. _____ Her purple barn in the meadow will be the dance hall.

3. _____ Our dragon was angry about the rain.

4. _____ A spotlight seems bright for that scene.

5. _____ Mr. McCall's stallion was a race horse in Kentucky.

6. _____ During art class, a bee was the subject of my drawing.

7. _____ Those pink and purple petunias appear perfect for the party.

8. _____ Rory and Alexandra were friends before kindergarten.

9. _____ Whose blue shoes are clean after a run?

10. ____ That superhero with the helmet is an accountant.

11. ____ Our skills on the unicycle are decent.

12. ____ The octopus in the bowler was a drummer for the band.

Linking Verbs
Predicate Nominatives and Adjectives

Directions: Draw a line through <u>prepositional phrases</u>. Underline the <u>simple subject</u> once and <u>linking verbs</u> twice. Label any <u>predicate adjectives</u> as **PA**. Label any <u>predicate nominatives</u> as **PN**.

                                                                                             PA
Examples: At two, we are good.   ➔   <s>At two,</s> <u>we</u> <u><u>are</u></u> **good**.
                                                                                               PN
                     We are cats in the play.   ➔   <u>We</u> <u><u>are</u></u> **cats** <s>in the play</s>.

1. _____ The tiger with the bow becomes calm.

2. _____ Our neighbor was a pilot in the Air Force.

3. _____ His pajamas will be more comfortable after the wash.

4. _____ Potato and Jelly are the names of our dogs.

5. _____ Between two ferns, the bearded man seemed strange.

6. _____ A takeout container in the fridge smells rotten.

7. _____ The robot on the scooter is our new tutor.

8. _____ My new chicken at the farm stays hungry during the day.

9. _____ In college, my majors were economics and German.

10. ____ Those diligent students will be leaders of tomorrow.

11. ____ Mayor Acorn remains confident and calm in the meeting.

12. ____ The penguin's friend at school was a tree frog.

Transitive Verbs / Intransitive Verbs
NOTES

Verbs
Transitive and Intransitive

A. Directions: Each of the following sentences contains a <u>transitive verb</u>. Underline the verbs twice and circle the first object (noun) that follows them.

Examples: The man threw a ball to a dog. →
The man <u>threw</u> a (ball) to a dog.

1. A delivery man pushes the door.

2. Our oldest robot washes our spaceship.

3. Ricardo's salamander eats many flies.

4. The children play a game of chess.

5. During campouts, we roast marshmallows by the fire.

B. Directions: Underline the <u>simple subject</u> once and the <u>verbs</u> twice. If the verb is <u>transitive</u>, write a <u>T</u> in the blank. If <u>intransitive</u>, write an <u>I</u>.

Examples: ___ She lit a match. → <u>T</u> <u>She</u> <u>lit</u> a match.
___ He drives fast. → <u>I</u> <u>He</u> <u>drives</u> fast.

1. ____ The boy in blue goes to that school.

2. ____ A pitcher throws a ball toward the catcher.

3. ____ Mark Patel draws pictures on his notebook

4. ____ Our donkeys were extras in the movie.

5. ____ At the talent show, that girl lifted a car!

Verbs
Transitive and Intransitive

A. Directions: Underline the simple subject once and the verbs twice. If the verb is transitive, write a **T** in the blank. If intransitive, write an **I**.

Examples: ___ The dogs ate rapidly. → **I** The dogs ate rapidly.
___ We bought a tiny cup. → **T** We bought a tiny cup.

1. ____ The artists painted trees on the wall.

2. ____ Mrs. Willikers drives to the store.

3. ____ My cousin drives his motorbike through the desert.

4. ____ This cow with stripes is a very fast runner.

5. ____ Two scouts flew the new rocket to Mars.

B. Directions: Draw a line through any prepositional phrases. Underline the simple subject once, verbs twice, and label any direct object as **DO**.

Examples: The lady gave a toy to her kid. →   **DO**
The lady gave a **toy** to her kid.

1. The artists painted trees on the wall.

2. Mrs. Willikers drives to the store.

3. My cousin drives his motorbike through the desert.

4. This cow with stripes is a very fast runner.

5. Two scouts flew the new rocket to Mars.

**Transitive Verbs
Direct Objects**

Directions: Draw a line through any prepositional phrases. Underline the simple subject once, verbs twice, and label the direct objects as **DO** .

Examples: The lady gave a toy to her kid. ➔   **DO**
The lady gave a **toy** to her kid.

1. The student raised her hand during English class.

2. Yesterday, Bilal took the train to Chattanooga.

3. The lady in boots played drums and guitar at the festival.

4. Across the galaxy, they mined big diamonds on an asteroid.

5. The gnomes carried their hopes and dreams in their hearts.

6. She mowed lawns at golf courses for extra money.

7. Roberto's step-daughter bought a new iguana from a zoo.

8. That dragon with all the treasure stole my baseball card.

9. Our neighbor grows tomatoes in her garden.

10. Naomi drove over the bridge and bought a kite.

11. A boy with freckles taught his teacher a lesson.

12. At the game, he threw the ball and hit a tree.

Transitive Verbs
Direct Objects

Directions: Draw a line through any <u>prepositional phrases</u>. Underline the <u>simple subject</u> once and the <u>verbs</u> twice. If the verb is <u>transitive</u>, write a <u>T</u> in the blank and circle the <u>direct object</u>.

Examples: ___ Men walk to work. → ___ Men <u>walk</u> <s>to work</s>.

___ At ten, we took a nap. → <u>T</u> <s>At ten,</s> <u>we</u> <u>took</u> a (nap).

1. ____ The pelicans on the pier ate twenty fish.

2. ____ Did you donate any money in the fundraiser?

3. ____ Our mom drove to the store for pancake batter.

4. ____ Throw the football to the wide receiver.

5. ____ After the movie, I ran to my house.

6. ____ Those players in green left the field after practice.

7. ____ Dr. Patel works at a veterinary clinic near the airport.

8. ____ Who gave the blanket to the neighbor's dog?

9. ____ Some musicians from Athens drove into town.

10. ____ Otters at the zoo played in their habitat.

11. ____ During the flight, the pilot gave a history lesson on the intercom.

12. ____ The bank on Main Street gave a loan to the new owners.

Direct Objects / Indirect Objects
NOTES

Transitive Verbs
Direct Objects and Indirect Object

A. Directions: Underline the simple subject once and the transitive verbs twice. Circle the direct object.

Examples: She gave a gift. → She gave a (gift)

1. Seymour took that football.

2. The new teacher threw an apple.

3. Our pet poodle gave a speech.

4. A famous artist drew a picture.

5. Those steel workers make cars.

B. Directions: Underline the simple subject once and the transitive verbs twice. Circle the direct object. Put a box around the indirect object.

Examples: She gave Jane a gift. → She gave [Jane] a (gift)

1. Seymour took the quarterback that football.

2. The new teacher threw Molly an apple.

3. Our pet poodle gave my class a speech.

4. A famous artist drew our mom a picture.

5. Those steel workers make us cars.

Transitive Verbs
Direct Objects and Indirect Object

A. Directions: Draw a line through prepositional phrases. Underline the simple subject once and the transitive verbs twice. Circle the direct object.

　　Examples:　　In class, he taught a lesson. ➔
　　　　　　　　~~In class~~, he taught a(lesson)

1. The otter threw a party in the pond.

2. On Tuesday, Mr. Petrovic gave a pop quiz.

3. Their yak with a Mohawk stole a cupcake.

4. Did Stan and Ollie win a gold medal?

5. Take a flower after the pageant.

B. Directions: Draw a line through prepositional phrases. Underline the simple subject once and the transitive verbs twice. Circle the direct object. Put a box around the indirect object.

　　Examples:　　In class, he taught his dog a lesson. ➔
　　　　　　　　~~In class~~, he taught his [dog] a(lesson)

1. The otter threw his friends a party in the pond.

2. On Tuesday, Mr. Petrovic gave my fish a pop quiz.

3. Their yak with a Mohawk stole me a cupcake.

4. Did Stan and Ollie win Mom a gold medal?

5. Take Cletus a flower after the pageant.

**Transitive Verbs
Direct Objects and Indirect Object**

Directions: Draw a line through any prepositional phrases. Underline the simple subject once and the transitive verbs twice. Label the direct object as **DO**. Label the indirect object as **IO**.

Example: A man at sea sold Akiva a fish. →   IO   DO
                                        A man ~~at sea~~ sold Akiva a fish.

1. During breakfast, Casper offered Faheem an orange.

2. The goat in the bowtie made us a ham sandwich.

3. Did my favorite teacher give my sister my homework?

4. That skeleton threw his dog a Frisbee in the park.

5. Catalina and Ha-joon loaned our class their hamster.

6. A spider caught her babies some flies on her web.

7. At halftime, the soccer player kicked the referee the ball

8. Bring your grandma a bouquet of flowers for her birthday.

9. Her niece in Oregon brought her an obsidian shard.

10. Do you buy your dog presents for her birthday?

11. After the first of May, we offer travelers free water.

12. Ellery stole himself a giant diamond from the museum.

13. The aliens gifted the humans new technology for their survival.

14. My grandma gave us a new quilt for our guest house.

Transitive Verbs
Direct Objects and Indirect Object

Directions: Draw a line through any prepositional phrases. Underline the simple subject once and the verbs twice. If* there is a direct object, label it as **DO**. If** there is an indirect object, label it as **IO**.

Example: Bill gave me tacos with beans. →   IO   DO
                                                            Bill gave me tacos ~~with beans~~.

1. The library loaned every student in my class a new laptop.

2. Our horses run quickly through the field near our farm.

3. Those robots gave me a high-five after the game.

4. Water the plants in the backyard during your next break.

5. Do I take my money to the bank?

6. The scientist caught us a butterfly for our assignment.

7. Jupiter gave a bone to his dog at the dog park.

8. Tymon and Abebe made their mom a necklace with seashells.

9. Take her the bag of cookies in the pantry.

10. The kids traded their desserts with their friends.

11. Has your cat brought you any dead birds in the past week?

12. At the ceremony, Ms. Martinez presented Isla a huge trophy.

* not every sentence will have a direct object
** not every sentence will have an indirect object

Helping Verbs List

to do	to have	(Modal Verbs)			to be		
do	has	may	could	can	am	was	be
does	have	might	should	will	is	were	being
did	had	must	would	shall	are		been

Helping (Auxiliary) Verbs
NOTES

Helping (Auxiliary) Verbs
NOTES

Verbs
Helping Verbs/Verb Phrases

A. Directions: The helping verbs in the following sentences have been underlined twice. Write a main verb in each blank to complete the sentence.

   Example: I may have _____ to school. →
              I may have **walked** to school.

1. The tiger might be _____ to the ice cream parlor._____

2. My basket should not have been _____ on the top shelf.

3. On Tuesday, can we be _____ at the beach?

4. Uncle Bob's pirate kittens have _____ off their bikes.

5. Sons of the groundhogs will be _____ at school.

B. Directions: Each example below contains a verb phrase. Underline all of the verbs twice. Circle the main verb.

   Example: She has not been running home. →
              She has not been running home.

1. Did my sister go to the movies with friends?

2. After a minute or two, they should be going.

3. In the morning, I shall wear my brand new suit.

4. Those squirrels must not have been eating the bird seed.

5. Were two girl in slippers climbing the stairs?

Verbs
Helping Verbs/Verb Phrases

A. Directions: The following sentences contain <u>helping verbs</u>. Write a <u>main verb</u> in each blank to complete the sentence, then underline the <u>verb phrases</u> twice.

    Example: He will be _____ to a park. →
                              He <u>will be</u> **<u>driving</u>** to a park.

1. Those panthers must have been _____ in the shadows.

2. A red kite with no string might have _____ away.

3. Would Mr. Elliot have _____ us candy from Japan?

4. During the day, I shouldn't be _____ to the aquarium.

5. Our new kitten was _____ strangely in the hall.

B. Directions: Each example below contains a <u>verb phrase</u>. Underline all of the <u>verbs</u> twice. Circle the <u>main verb</u>.

    Example: She has been running home. →
                              She <u>has been running</u> home.

1. A cobra could have been hiding in that old basket.

2. Will Gilda's robot butler be cleaning the chimney in the morning?

3. I am not allowed in the garden maze after my lessons.

4. Those students couldn't have been studying harder for finals.

5. The clock on the wall can be slow.

Verbs
Helping Verbs/Verb Phrases

Directions: Draw a line through any <u>prepositional phrases</u>. Underline the <u>simple subjects</u> once and the <u>verb phrases</u> twice. Circle the <u>main verb</u>.

   Example: My cat with spots might be going. →
                              My cat ~~with spots~~ might be going.

1. In the future, we will fly to the moon for vacation.

2. Is Talia's hairdo falling flat in the humidity?

3. Your mom and her cousin aren't going on the swamp tour.

4. I shall arrive at the party by midnight.

5. That capybara can be noisy before lunch.

6. Does King Petunia have water in his bowl?

7. Three of the hyenas must have been laughing at the moon.

8. A girl at the movies was being loud during the film

9. Kiko and Beverly couldn't have left the country.

10. Can our marching band play at the halftime show?

11. Little puppies were climbing into the box on the rug.

12. Her new markers should have plenty of ink.

13. The humongous python must have been dancing the samba.

14. After work, I am going to a concert with some old friends.

15. They might have been treading quietly on the grass.

Verbs
Helping Verbs/Verb Phrases

Directions: Draw a line through any prepositional phrases. Underline the simple subjects once and the verbs twice. **Not every sentence has a verb phrase.**

Example: Umi's dog may have been sleeping at home. →
Umi's <u>dog</u> <u><u>may have been sleeping</u></u> ~~at home~~.

1. The driver left and may have taken the car with him.

2. Must we work until 3 o'clock in the morning?

3. My favorite radio station will be playing my request in 5 minutes.

4. The nannies have not worked for three weeks.

5. Our neighbor's junk yard might be selling to the city soon.

6. Mr. Darcy doesn't need a piñata for his birthday party.

7. Am I taking the test in the gym today?

8. The koalas won't need lessons for the guitar.

9. Dryden and Vladimir were sledding down the hill.

10. After the trip to the museum, we will be eating lunch.

11. The kid with the propeller hat did not take the quiz.

12. Emmylou's parrot might have been eating crackers in its cage.

13. Those cookies aren't baked with raisins or chocolate chips.

14. Have any of our players gone to the game yet?

15. They could have flown to the Cayman Islands.

Verbs
Helping Verbs/Verb Phrases

Directions: Draw a line through any prepositional phrases. Underline the simple subjects once and the verbs twice. **Not every sentence has a verb phrase.**

   Example: During class, I may have fallen asleep. →
          ~~During class~~, I may have fallen asleep.

1. My mustang isn't eating her oats in the morning.

2. Did their grandma visit them this summer?

3. During the full moon, a wolf might have been howling.

4. Our twenty-three chinchillas could not escape from the cage.

5. Cassandra would have been a better choice for class president.

6. Will your sister be joining us on the tour of the White House?

7. The globe with the wooden base could sell for millions.

8. Three quail were crossing the street with their babies.

9. The dinosaur is not playing softball in the park today.

10. Students in my class should have been studying harder.

11. Her favorite movie theater will be closing for renovations.

12. Can you please practice your juggling in the backyard?

13. A snake has been sleeping in our backyard since last night.

14. Aren't you completing your homework at the library?

15. We drove to the coast and flew a kite on the beach.

**Verbs
Infinitives**

A. Directions: The following sentences contain <u>infinitive verbs</u>. Draw a line through <u>prepositional phrases</u>, underline the <u>simple subject</u> once, <u>verbs</u> twice, and circle the <u>infinitive verbs</u>.

> Example: He may try to take the quiz after school. →
>
> He <u>may try</u> ⊙to take⊙ the quiz ~~after school~~.

1. My kids asked to take the dirt buggy to the store.

2. In five minutes, I will want to take a break.

3. Ms. Monet's harpsichord needs to move up the stairs.

4. Proud fathers will have to stand up to see their children.

5. Ghosts in the mansion could need to move to Florida.

B. Directions: Draw a line through <u>prepositional phrases</u>, underline the <u>simple subject</u> once, <u>verbs</u> twice, and put parenthesis around the <u>infinitive verbs</u>. **not every sentence contains an infinitive verb**

> Example: At camp, she wanted to paddle canoes. →
>
> ~~At camp~~, <u>she</u> <u>wanted</u> **(**to paddle**)** canoes.

1. My favorite circus dog will go to sleep in the meadow.

2. In the summer, I am going to band camp.

3. Each of our trees sends their seeds to the wind.

4. Beauregard wants to give a tea party for the workers.

5. Do you want to travel to the Azores with me?

Verbs
NOTES

**Verbs
Contractions**

Directions: Draw a line connecting the pairs of words on the left to their matching <u>contractions</u> on the right.

1. **he + will**   a. **wasn't**

2. **will + not**   b. **there's**

3. **she + is**   c. **you'll**

4. **would + have**   d. **he'll**

5. **should + not**   e. **won't**

6. **they + are**   f. **hadn't**

7. **did + not**   g. **can't**

8. **was + not**   h. **you'll**

9. **I + am**   i. **I'm**

10. **there + is**   j. **she's**

11. **you + will**   k. **shouldn't**

12. **how + did**   l. **they're**

13. **cannot**   m. **would've**

14. **had + not**   n. **didn't**

15. **it + is**   o. **how'd**

**Verbs
Contractions**

Directions: In the blank, write the contraction for the two words that are given.

Examples: she + will = _____ → she + will = ___she'll___

did + not = _____ → did + not = ___didn't___

1. he + will = _____

2. they + will = _____

3. have + not = _____

4. would + have = _____

5. should + not = _____

6. I + will = _____

7. does + not = _____

8. is + not = _____

9. when + is = _____

10. she + would = _____

11. you + will = _____

12. must + not = _____

13. could + not = _____

14. had + not = _____

15. cannot = _____

16. you + are = _____

17. it + is = _____

18. he + is = _____

19. they + are = _____

20. how + did = _____

21. I + would = _____

22. it + is = _____

23. let + us = _____

24. that + will = _____

25. I + am = _____

26. there + is = _____

27. will + not = _____

28. they + would = _____

Verbs
Confusing Contractions

A. Directions: Circle the correct word (*its* or *it's*) to fill in the blank and complete each sentence. Pay attention to the spelling.

1. The robot took (it's , **its**) _____ dog to the vet.

2. I don't have the book, but (**it's** , its) _____ on the desk.

3. (**It's** , Its) _____ very cold in Antarctica.

4. (It's , **Its**) _____ paint was ruined after the accident.

B. Directions: Circle the correct word (*your* or *you're*) to fill in the blank and complete each sentence. Pay attention to the spelling.

1. My favorite author will sign books at (**your**, you're) _____ school.

2. (Your , **You're**) _____ the best mechanic in the shop.

3. If you continue to try, (your , **you're**) _____ going to succeed.

4. (**Your** , You're) _____ new sweater shrunk in the wash.

C. Directions: Circle the correct word (*there*, *their*, or *they're*) to fill in the blank and complete each sentence. Pay attention to the spelling.

1. (There , Their , **They're**) _____ going to the aquarium soon.

2. Did you return (there , **their** , they're) _____ cake pan?

3. (**There** , Their , They're) _____ are no more costumes.

4. You can go (**there** , their , they're) _____ tomorrow.

Verbs
Confusing Contractions

Directions: Circle the correct word to fill in the blank and complete each sentence. Pay attention to the spelling.

1. (Your , You're) _____ an excellent student.

2. I went (there , their , they're) _____ after the air show.

3. My android left because (it's , its) _____ going to a movie.

4. (There , Their , They're) _____ horse eats apples and oats.

5. Mr. Marlowe solved (your, you're) _____ mystery.

6. I think that (there , their , they're) _____ joining us.

7. Our pizza lost (it's , its) _____ pepperoni on the trip.

8. (There , Their , They're) _____ the best wrestlers in the state.

9. (It's , Its) _____ too cold to play baseball at the park.

10. Ms. Diaz said that (your, you're) _____ flying to Spain.

11. If we lose our hats in the ocean, (it's , its) _____ your fault.

12. (Your , You're) _____ camera takes wonderful pictures.

13. (There , Their , They're) _____ are too many daisies.

14. The factory is losing (it's , its) _____ power supply.

15. Did (there , their , they're) _____ car get washed?

16. Coley's motorcycle is in (your, you're) _____ garage.

Verbs
NOTES

Verbs
Irregular Past Tense

A. Directions: In the blank, write the past tense form of the infinitive verb that is given. If the past tense form of the verb is irregular, circle it.

Examples: (to pull) _____ → (to pull) __pulled__
(to drive) _____ → (to drive) (drove)

1. (to lock) _____
2. (to find) _____
3. (to hop) _____
4. (to cut) _____
5. (to leave) _____

6. (to give) _____
7. (to escape) _____
8. (to wear) _____
9. (to go) _____
10. (to try) _____

B. Directions: In the blank, write the irregular past tense form of the infinitive verb that is given to complete each sentence.

Examples: (to run) Yesterday, I _____ to school.
→ (to run) Yesterday, I __ran__ to school.

1. (to buy) We _____ tickets three week ago.

2. (to fly) During a recent vacation, they _____ kites in a park.

3. (to make) Grandma _____ apple pie last Thanksgiving.

4. (to do) _____ you go to the movies yesterday?

5. (to take) Two years ago, I _____ a train cross-country.

Verbs
Irregular Past Tense

Directions: Circle the correct <u>past tense</u> form, and write that word in the blank.

    Examples: Bob (knew , knowed) _____ the answer.
    →   Bob (knew , knowed) <u>*knew*</u> the answer.

1. The author (writed , wrote) _____ me a letter.

2. After lunch, a bell (ringed , rang) _____ in the cafeteria.

3. That large crane (breaked , broke) _____ from the weight.

4. Mrs. Shapiro's scissors (cut , cutted) _____ the paper.

5. We (taught , teached) _____ our dog a new trick.

6. In Alaska, the rivers (freezed , froze) _____ in October.

7. His students (taked , took) _____ their final exam.

8. That salesperson already (speaked , spoke) _____ to us.

9. Our choir (singed , sang) _____ at the state fair.

10. Ricardo (bought , buyed) _____ video games at the mall.

11. The bonsai trees (growed , grew) _____ slowly.

12. My detectives (finded , found) _____ a new clue.

13. Yesterday, the sun (rised , rose) _____ a 6:23am.

14. A performer (blew , blowed) _____ bubbles at the park.

15. The gray cat (sleeped , slept) _____ in the sun.

Verbs
Irregular Past Participle

Directions: In the blank, write the irregular past particle form of the infinitive verb that is given to complete each sentence. Next, underline the verb phrase twice (helping verbs and the main verb in the blank).

   Example: **(to eat)** We had _____ lunch already.
   ➔   **(to eat)** We <u>had eaten</u> lunch already.

1. **(to write)** The journalist has _____ a new article.

2. **(to fly)** Our spaceship had _____ to Mars already.

3. **(to sink)** Lots of ships have _____ in the Pacific Ocean.

4. **(to come)** The time has _____ to return to our cabins.

5. **(to begin)** Mr. Stravinsky has _____ to play harmonica.

6. **(to lie)** Two dogs had _____ on the new sofa.

7. **(to steal)** Some cat burglars have _____ the jewels.

8. **(to throw)** The gorilla has _____ the beach ball.

9. **(to leave)** An Elvis impersonator has _____ the building.

10. **(to go)** They had _____ to the concert two hours early.

11. **(to shake)** I have _____ the hands of kings and queens.

12. **(to wear)** A man on TV had _____ a plaid suit.

13. **(to rise)** The sun has _____ in the eastern sky.

14. **(to run)** Every student _____ during P.E.

15. **(to buy)** Our grandfather _____ a skateboard.

Verbs
Irregular Past Participle

Directions: Underline the simple subject once. Circle the correct past participle from the options given, and then underline the verb phrase twice.

Examples: We had (did , done) _____ our homework.
→ We had (did , done) _____ our homework.

1. Our new teacher has (taught , teached) _____ at a university.

2. Those lollipops might have (been , were) _____ in my pocket.

3. Soldiers have (sweared , sworn) _____ an oath to their country.

4. My little brother has (breaked , broken) _____ his arm.

5. Her students had (hung , hanged) _____ decorations on the wall.

6. The emperor has (spoken , spoke) _____ to many advisors.

7. Mrs. Kobayashi may have (driven , drove) _____ a racecar.

8. The Cubs had (beat , beaten) _____ the Cardinals on Tuesday.

9. Those archaeologists have (found , finded) _____ a tomb.

10. My grandparents have (sitted , sat) _____ on many porches.

11. Our chickens have (laid , lain) _____ many eggs this year.

12. Scholars have (known , knew) _____ this fact for decades.

13. Olga's pencil had (fell, fallen) _____ off of her desk.

14. His dad had (set , setted) _____ his watch ahead 5 minutes.

15. George could have (got , gotten) _____ a new hatchet.

Descriptive (How) Adverbs
NOTES

Adverbs
Descriptive (How?)

Directions: In the blank, write the <u>adverb</u> form for the adjective that is given.

Examples: swift _____ → swift ___*swiftly*___
fast _____ → fast ___*fast*___

1. slow _____
2. rough _____
3. nervous _____
4. good _____
5. silent _____
6. kind _____
7. brave _____
8. careful _____
9. bad _____
10. truthful _____
11. respectful _____
12. awkward _____
13. quiet _____
14. delightful _____

15. angry _____
16. sleepy _____
17. tired _____
18. complete _____
19. eager _____
20. secure _____
21. gleeful _____
22. bright _____
23. noisy _____
24. hesitant _____
25. excellent _____
26. peaceful _____
27. happy _____
28. rapid _____

Adverbs
Descriptive (How?)

Directions: Read the first sentence and identify the <u>adjective</u> in **bold**. Write the <u>adverb</u> form for it in the blank to complete the second sentence.

Example: The knight was **brave**. She fought _____.
→ The knight was **brave**. She fought _bravely_.

1. Her hamster was **noisy**. He moved _____ in his cage.

2. My mom seems **sleepy**. This morning, she arose _____.

3. The mouse was totally **silent**. It crept _____ in the kitchen.

4. That car is very **slow**. It is _____ cruising down the street.

5. Our student is **sloppy** writer. He writes _____ on tests.

6. This rabbit is so **quick**. She runs _____ through the field.

7. Their grandma is **kind**. She treats everyone _____.

8. Peter is a **good** surfer. He surfs very _____.

9. Your clothing seems **loose**. It hangs _____ on your body.

10. My brother can be **awkward**. He behaves _____ at times.

11. The vault appears **secure**. It will _____ guard the loot.

12. That dog sounds **furious**. He's barking _____ at birds.

13. This spaceship is **solid**. It was built _____ by engineers.

14. We have **fancy** clothes. We dress _____ and dance.

15. Mohinder is **quiet**. He sits _____ in his seat.

Adverbs
Descriptive (How?)

A. Directions: Read the <u>adjective</u> in **bold** and write its <u>adverb</u> form in the blank to complete the sentence.

Example: **(quiet)** The ninjas snuck _____ into the barn.
→ **(quiet)** The ninjas snuck ___*quietly*___ into the barn.

1. **(noisy)** The aliens slithered _____ on the roof.

2. **(sleepy)** A sloth climbed _____ along the branch.

3. **(eager)** Some girl scouts _____ sold cookies.

4. **(brave)** Her dog _____ swam across the river.

5. **(good)** Uncle Sven did _____ on his civics assignment.

6. **(bad)** My dinosaurs performed _____ in the dance battle.

7. **(fast)** Her jet flew _____ across the sky.

8. **(loud)** Our neighbors party _____ on Labor Day.

9. **(aggressive)** The gerbil _____ guarded her den.

10. **(free)** Their governor gave her permission _____.

11. **(sour)** Grandpa looked _____ at his broken tractor.

12. **(dry)** A comedian _____ joked about my haircut.

13. **(hard)** Mr. Tangles tried _____ to build a time machine.

14. **(dutiful)** His nurse _____ changed his bandage.

15. **(awkward)** She danced _____ with the troll.

Adverbs
Descriptive (How?)

Directions: Write any descriptive <u>adverb</u> that you choose in each the blanks to complete each sentence.

    Example: A dinosaur walked _____ into the museum.
    ➔   A dinosaur walked <u>*loudly*</u> into the museum.

1. The superhero flew _____ toward the battle.

2. A snow owl sits _____ on the branch.

3. Our candles with stripes are burning _____.

4. Mr. Chaudhary wrote _____ about the album.

5. That cameraperson _____ runs into trouble.

6. My Aunt Maria sings _____ in the shower.

7. The new drummer in the school band plays _____.

8. We argue _____ at student council meetings.

9. Those chickens peck _____ at their feed.

10. Ms. Ndobo _____ drives to work.

11. Her son _____ digs in his sandbox.

12. Some kittens are _____ playing on the bed.

13. Few elves shoot arrows _____ in the woods.

14. An entire parade marched _____ down the street.

15. The saxophone player played _____ with the band.

**Adverbs
NOTES**

Adverbs
NOTES

**Adverbs
When?**

Directions: Read the sentences and circle the <u>adverbs</u> that answer the question: <u>when</u>(?).

Example: Susan swims in the ocean today. →
                       Susan sits by the pool (today)

1. The Smiths recently bought a new car.

2. My favorite teacher practices yoga daily.

3. The train from Santa Fe will arrive late.

4. Have you ever flown a kite?

5. Sometimes our robot visits the shop for a tune-up.

6. My mother would never give me a sugary cereal.

7. We occasionally take field trips to the university.

8. Visit your grandparents soon.

9. Mr. Berrycloth frequently walks to the park.

10. Today, a pirate will put on a fashion show.

11. Office workers may often take breaks at their desks.

12. His beard was now weird.

13. Tonight, my tennis club is having a party.

14. Those birds should have woken up sooner.

15. Alysa arrived yesterday after the concert.

**Adverbs
When?**

Directions: In the following sentences, write an <u>adverb</u> in each of the blanks that answers the question: <u>when</u>(?).

Example: Tej _____ rides his bike. ➔
Tej ___*often*___ rides his bike.

1. My neighbor's car drives _____ on dirt roads.

2. Her goldfish _____ swims in its bowl.

3. Martha runs over the rainbow_____.

4. The pug in the tuxedo _____ dances.

5. They _____ ride their tandem bicycle.

6. The hawk flew _____ across the sky.

7. _____, a tractor plodded across the field.

8. The injured dancer should go to her room _____.

9. Rodrigo studies for his chemistry class _____.

10. We _____ go to the beach after school.

11. _____ the cats are fed at the neighbor's house.

12. The mail will be picked up _____ in the morning.

13. Did the school call _____ about your sister?

14. Go clean up your room _____.

15. We will _____ meet the Martians.

Adverbs
When?

Directions: In the following sentences, draw a line through any <u>prepositional phrases</u>, underline the <u>simple subjects</u> once, <u>verbs</u> twice, and circle any <u>adverb</u> that answers the question: <u>when</u>(?).

Example: We will soon go to a circus. →

We will (soon) go ~~to a circus~~.

1. We should buy our tickets soon.

2. Recently, some clowns marched through the supermarket.

3. Mr. Flamingo always washes his car on Sundays.

4. Will my grandparents arrive late?

5. That rainbow appeared suddenly in the sky.

6. Yesterday, the Kendi family had a party.

7. Does your mother go to the gym daily?

8. Our goats sometimes eat the neighbor's grass.

9. Milosz may join us tomorrow after his soccer practice.

10. They went to the store earlier before the show.

11. Kara and Jaleel will now take the stage.

12. The cactus garden has never looked so good.

13. My clothing rarely seems as fancy as yours.

**Adverbs
Where?**

Directions: Read the sentences and circle the <u>adverbs</u> that answer the question: <u>where</u>(?).

    Example: A bird flew by during lunch. →

                                      A bird flew (by) during lunch.

1. The dog went outside after he ate breakfast.

2. Her new hat was nearby on a coatrack.

3. I don't know for sure, but we're going somewhere.

4. Your backpack is there, beside the refrigerator.

5. She went inside to call her parents.

6. The parade with the huge floats marched downtown.

7. A large ship sailed away after the sunrise.

8. My grandmother went down into the basement.

9. Their spaceship flew forward through the hanger doors.

10. We rolled around in the snow.

11. Those baby otters play close to their den.

12. The magic carpet arrived, and the children climbed on.

13. If you climb in, the wagon can start rolling.

14. His hand went up, but the teacher didn't see it.

15. Suzie went there during her last trip to the chocolate factory.

Adverbs
Where?

Directions: In the following sentences, write an <u>adverb</u> in each of the blanks that answers the question: <u>where</u>(?).

Example: Raya runs_____ after school. ➔
                  Raya runs____*there*____ after school.

1. We are going _____ in the morning.

2. A bird flew _____ outside the window.

3. My uncle walked _____ for a magazine.

4. Renata is _____ beside the old clock.

5. The magic lamp fell _____, and we can't get it.

6. Her jacket is _____ on the hook.

7. Those chickens in the coop aren't going _____.

8. Sawdust is _____ in the workshop.

9. A rocket ship shot _____ to the stars.

10. My little sister ran _____ last summer.

11. That kangaroo jumped _____ of the trampoline.

12. The astronaut with the mustache floated _____.

13. Their circus toured _____ on this continent.

14. An orangutan climbed _____ on the swingset.

15. Clyde flies _____ in his helicopter.

**Adverbs
Where?**

Directions: In the following sentences, draw a line through any <u>prepositional phrases</u>, underline the <u>simple subjects</u> once, <u>verbs</u> twice, and circle any <u>adverb</u> that answers the question: <u>where</u>(?).

Example: They went up to the moon. →

They <u>went</u> (up) ~~to the moon~~.

1. The swimmer pushed away from the boat.

2. You should go outside and play in the sun.

3. Many of the teachers travel around in the summer.

4. Does the man with the roller skates live nearby?

5. Meg and her sister will be travelling there.

6. The puppies are running around in the yard.

7. Our guide rowed upstream in the old canoe.

8. Climb aboard and take your seat.

9. A rabbit jumped up onto the motorcycle.

10. We can't go anywhere during the school year.

11. After the light turns green, you can move forward.

12. Are your students going far for college?

13. At the public pool, they both fell in.

Adverbs
To What Extent?

Directions: Read the sentences and circle the <u>adverbs</u> that answer the question: <u>to what extent</u>(?).

Example: That popsicle is so cold. →
                         That popsicle is (so) cold.

1. The young boy was (quite) timid in the playground.

2. Our parents are (rather) sleepy after dinner.

3. A young dinosaur walks (somewhat) slowly in the forest.

4. Those musicians do (not) have a concert tonight.

5. A (very) excited puppy peed on the bedroom floor.

6. Grandma thought the comedian was (so) funny.

7. Did the ninja student sneak (too) noisily along the roof?

8. My toolbox has been (extremely) useful on our trip.

9. A (somewhat) sleepy kitten curled up in the blanket.

10. The hedges hadn't been trimmed for weeks.

11. Those trees are (totally) gnarly.

12. We could (barely) hear the birdsong in the meadow.

13. Mend the necklace on the counter (very) carefully.

14. That test in chemistry was (quite) confusing.

15. Tasha was (completely) prepared for the race.

Adverbs
To What Extent?

Directions: Read the sentences and circle the <u>adverbs</u> that answer the question: <u>to what extent</u>(?). Draw an arrow to the word it modifies. In the blank, write the type of word being modified: <u>verb</u>, <u>adverb</u>, or <u>adjective</u>.

Example: She ran too quickly. _____

→   She ran (too) quickly.   <u> adverb </u>

1. The guests need to stay very calm. _____

2. Carla's race car drove quite quickly. _____

3. Didn't we go to Mexico last year? _____

4. My teacher reads rather quietly. _____

5. That student film was so funny. _____

6. One squirrel completed the course pretty well. _____

7. Roderick could hardly believe his eyes. _____

8. Our annual party has become incredibly large. _____

9. Are all of the students laughing too loudly? _____

10. Do not go into the haunted house tonight. _____

11. That somewhat dim light bulb can be changed. _____

12. Uncle Jack could barely breathe after the hike. _____

13. He wrote his essay too sloppily. _____

Adverbs
To What Extent?

Directions: In each blank, write an <u>adverb</u> that answer the question: <u>to what extent</u>(?). Try not to reuse any adverbs.

Example: The car moved _____ fast. ➔
                       The car moved __*quite*__ fast.

1. Our summer break passed _____ quickly.

2. The new pilot acted _____ carelessly.

3. Mrs. Hannigan did _____ sweep the stairs.

4. That shop is _____ expensive for me.

5. A beautiful flamingo will be _____ photogenic.

6. Domingo was writing _____ neatly.

7. A new robot seems _____ useful.

8. They slept _____ peacefully at the cabin.

9. Her _____ fat cat sat on the windowsill.

10. The brilliant scientist could _____ begin the study.

11. My schedule is _____ full this weekend.

12. The chef became _____ angry last night.

13. Their _____ new car has leather seats.

14. Lulu had a _____ bad feeling about this.

15. We took a _____ fun tour in New Orleans.

**Adverbs
All Types**

Directions: In the following sentences, circle every example of an <u>adverb</u>. The number in parentheses tells how many adverbs are in the sentence.

Example: (4) A very fat dog ran too clumsily yesterday.

→ (4) A (very) fat dog ran (too) (clumsily) (yesterday).

1. (3) The taxi drove downtown too fast in the storm.

2. (2) A very hungry dog ate aggressively in the kitchen.

3. (3) My grandma travels everywhere and really enjoys eating well.

4. (3) That rather sweet boy is studying there in the library today.

5. (3) Soon, an extremely clever thief will simply steal the painting.

6. (2) Mr. Renaud rode his bike too close to the busy street.

7. (2) Our somewhat friendly dog runs to the park daily.

8. (3) They arrived late and swiftly built a campfire nearby.

9. (3) The mouse climbed in, and we did not run away.

10. (2) Mom arrived earlier, and she was incredibly happy.

11. (3) Those monkeys climb on gracefully and sometimes stay.

12. (3) His friends hang around and totally eat our really tasty food.

13. (3) Don't you go over to your grandma's house frequently?

14. (3) We never fly slowly in our spaceship, but we fly carefully.

Nominative Pronouns / Objective Pronouns
NOTES

Nominative Pronouns / Objective Pronouns
NOTES

Pronouns
Nominative

Directions: Read the first sentence and notice the underlined word(s). In the second sentence, write a <u>nominative pronoun</u> that could replace the underlined word(s) in the blank to complete the sentence.

Example: Mr. Diop has good hair. _____ has good hair.
→ Mr. Diop has good hair. ___He___ has good hair.

1. Mrs. Chopra will be an engineer. _____ will be an engineer.

2. Those cows look peaceful. _____ look peaceful.

3. (*your name*) is awesome! _____ am awesome!

4. The clock is broken. _____ is broken.

5. My cousin and I went to camp. _____ went to camp.

6. "Marjorie, _____ have ketchup on your new dress."

7. Yesterday, Curtis went shopping. Yesterday, _____ went shopping.

8. ??????? in the world are you? _____ in the world are you?

9. Dahlia is a girl. _____ is a girl.

10. This robot fixes old guitars. _____ fixes old guitars.

11. Nihal and I go fishing at the lake. _____ go fishing at the lake.

12. Our parents like to travel. _____ like to travel.

13. A fireman saved us! _____ saved us!

131

**Pronouns
Nominative**

Directions: In the following sentences, circle any nominative pronoun. In the blank, write an **S** if the pronoun is the *subject* or a **PN** if the pronoun is a *predicate nominative*.

Examples: I am a dog. ____   →   (I) am a dog. **S**
                    A doctor is she. ____   →   A doctor is (she). **PN**

1. The woman with the little dog in her purse was she. ____

2. After lunch, they went to the park. ____

3. I would like to visit a volcano someday. ____

4. That bag with the rainbow strap is it. ____

5. We never left the cabin last winter. ____

6. The masked super hero was you? ____

7. My sister and I drove ATVs on the beach. ____

8. Who were the cyclists with rainbow outfits? ____

9. Tomorrow, she will fly to Paris. ____

10. It's the holiday with the most greeting cards. ____

11. You and Henri were the last to arrive. ____

12. Her parents are they on the rollercoaster. ____

13. The dancing gorilla ninja was who?! ____

Pronouns
Nominative

Directions: In the following sentences, circle the correct <u>pronoun</u> to complete each sentence. In the blank, write an **S** if the pronoun is the *subject* or a **PN** if the pronoun is a *predicate nominative*.

Examples: Kara is (she / her). ____   →   Kara is ((she)/ her). **PN**
(I / Me) am afraid. ____   →   ((I)/ Me) am afraid. **S**

1. Did (they / them) leave the party? _____

2. The man with the long beard is (him / he). _____

3. (She / Her) will be the next governor of Texas. _____

4. The monster was (it / them) by the chocolate fountain. _____

5. (Who / Whom) was the belle of the ball? _____

6. Yesterday, (you / yous) hiked on Mt. Rainier. _____

7. The winner of the spelling bee was (me / I). _____

8. (Us / We) can cook a feast for our guests. _____

9. Allison and (her / she) drank milkshakes. _____

10. Some goblins and (they / them) had tea. _____

11. The coolest person in the world is (you / them). _____

12. Adam, Ella, and (him / he) took the clown car. _____

13. The slowest runners on the track were (we / us) at the back. _____

**Pronouns
Objective**

Directions: Read the first sentence and notice the underlined word(s). In the second sentence, write a <u>objective pronoun</u> that could replace the underlined word(s) in the blank to complete the sentence.

Example: He threw <u>the ball</u>. He threw _____.

→ He threw <u>the ball</u>. He threw ___*it*___.

1. Jennica gave <u>Monica</u> a hug. Jennica gave _____ a hug.

2. She gave <u>her wallet</u> to Tan. She gave _____ to Tan.

3. To <u>??????</u> did you throw a party? To _____ did you throw a party?

4. Our family lives near <u>Walter</u>. Our family lives near _____.

5. Come to the beach with <u>Kel and me</u>. Come to the beach with _____.

6. <u>(*your friend's name*)</u>, did _____ select your classes yet?

7. The android gave <u>our dogs</u> a treat. The android gave _____ a treat.

8. <u>I</u> want to take my stuffed animals to camp with _____.

9. A turtle crawled to <u>Martha</u>. A turtle crawled to _____.

10. Mr. Moody took <u>the train</u> to Bern. Mr. Moody took _____ to Bern.

11. We will go with Casey and <u>Kyle</u>. We will go with Casey and _____.

12. It fell between Nan and <u>Raj and me</u>. It fell between Nan and _____.

13. Liza took <u>her kids</u> to the zoo. Liza took _____ to the zoo.

Pronouns
Objective

Directions: In the following sentences, circle any <u>objective pronoun</u>. In the blank, write an **OP** if the pronoun is the *object of the preposition,* a **DO** if the pronoun is a *direct object*, or an **IO** if the pronoun is an *indirect object*.

Examples: We went with him. ____   ➔   We went with (him) **OP**
                     I gave them toys. ____   ➔   I gave (them) toys. **IO**

1. Martin gave a coupon to her. _____

2. The Martians loaned them a new pickaxe. _____

3. Take me to the mountain lake. _____

4. Did the sasquatch follow us to the cabin? _____

5. For whom did you buy that cuckoo clock? _____

6. We gave it a bath before lunch. _____

7. The warning was for him. _____

8. One final treasure is hidden between the flag and you. _____

9. A swamp creature gave John and her some seeds. _____

10. For them, the taco is the perfect food. _____

11. I want to take you to the museum. _____

12. The kittens in the field ran toward us. _____

13. That lady saved me from the fire. _____

Pronouns
Nominative and Objective

Directions: In the following sentences, circle the correct pronoun to complete each sentence. In the blank, write an **S** if the pronoun is the *subject* or a **PN** if the pronoun is a *predicate nominative*. Write an **OP** if the pronoun is the *object of the preposition*, a **DO** if the pronoun is a *direct object*, or an **IO** if the pronoun is an *indirect object*.

Examples: Jill likes (she / her). _____ → Jill likes (she /(her)). **DO**
(I / Me) love fun! _____ → ((I)/ Me) love fun! **S**

1. The man in the pork pie hat is (he / him) _____

2. Do you want to go with (he / him)? _____

3. (They / Them) are the best dinosaur hunters. _____

4. Take (they / them) to the cleaners. _____

5. The fairies gave (we / us) magical powers. _____

6. (I / Me) want a cookie. _____

7. Marcia bought (she / her) the puppet. _____

8. The owner of that mansion is (who / whom)? _____

9. A massive wave carried (we / us) to shore. _____

10. (Who / Whom) forgot to bring a pencil? _____

11. To (who / whom) did you give your money? _____

12. The winner of the last game was (I , me). _____

Possessive Pronouns / Reflexive Pronouns
NOTES

**Pronouns
Possessive**

Directions: In the following sentences, circle any <u>possessive pronoun</u> and draw an arrow to the noun that it modifies/possesses.

Examples: I have her book.   →   I have (her) book.
            Dad took our car.   →   Dad took (our) car.

1. My hat is on the hook in the hallway.

2. I gave Mr. Foley his cowboy hat.

3. Whose ham is this?

4. It was her medal after the race.

5. They wanted to go to their ranch for the winter.

6. Your old scooter sits under the elm tree.

7. Jan and Shuri went to our school for the carnival.

8. If the robot rusts, its gears won't work.

9. That cartoon character wants to steal your sister's lunch.

10. Their new pool table was delivered to them yesterday.

11. We went to my favorite camping spot over the weekend.

12. Helena went to her room so she could do her homework.

13. Our family visited Elvis, and we stayed at his house.

14. Whose empty picnic basket is this?

15. The house lost its roof in the storm.

Pronouns
Possessive

Directions: In the following sentences, write any <u>possessive pronoun</u> (my, mine, his, her, hers, your, yours, its our, ours, their, theirs, whose) that makes sense into the blank to finish the sentence. Try to use all of them.

    Examples: The cat is _____. ➔ The cat is <u>*mine*</u>.
                          Bud has _____ keys. ➔ Bud has <u>*his*</u> keys.

1. I want to ride _____ bike to the park.

2. _____ new car is in the driveway.

3. _____ backpack is sitting on the counter.

4. The cherry pie on the windowsill is _____.

5. That house will be _____, after they sign the papers.

6. Is _____ record player still working?

7. Last summer, we went to _____ grandma's house.

8. The guitar on the wall is missing one of _____ strings.

9. Any dessert will be _____, if you answer the riddle.

10. _____ old t-shirts would make a soft blanket.

11. Do you know _____ seat this is?

12. Mrs. Adeyemi brought us _____ famous casserole.

13. A lot of these recipes are _____.

**Pronouns
Possessive**

Directions: In the following sentences, circle any <u>possessive pronoun</u> and draw an arrow back to its <u>antecedent(s)</u>.

    Examples: Al likes his teacher.   →   Al likes (his) teacher.
                         We ate our lunch.   →   We ate (our) lunch.

1. Barbara forgot her sunglass at the beach.

2. That bookstore opens its doors in thirty minutes.

3. We will be flying our new rocket ship tomorrow.

4. You are the master of your own destiny.

5. John Henry carried his hammer to the tent.

6. Sela and Nat went home to their apartment.

7. The old lady polished her sword before the battle.

8. Some robot left its bowtie at the concert.

9. Those pelicans are looking for their next meal.

10. Jessica and I will be leaving our games here.

11. Uncle Ibrahim forgot his reading glasses.

12. Auntie Anya loaned him her extra pair.

13. Mr. Volk, is this your coffee mug?

14. The baseball players went into their dugout.

15. Our school sits on top of a huge hill.

**Pronouns
Reflexive**

Directions: In the following sentences, circle any <u>reflexive pronoun</u> and draw an arrow back to its <u>antecedent(s)</u>.

Examples: Jojo fixed it himself.   →   Jojo fixed it himself.

1. Hazel, herself, was excited about the rain.

2. They want to bake the cake by themselves.

3. Do you want to explore the country yourself?

4. Castor and I will teach them ourselves.

5. I hope to fly myself across the universe.

6. The teachers themselves were happy about the rain.

7. He helped himself to a second helping of cake.

8. The Johnsons planned the heist themselves.

9. My robot took itself to the mechanic.

10. After graduation, I will treat myself to a European vacation.

11. We left early and put ourselves to bed.

12. The house itself survived the hurricane.

Pronouns
Pronoun or Adjective?

Directions: In the following sentences, decide whether the word in italics is behaving as a <u>pronoun</u> or as a <u>limiting adjective</u>. If it's a pronoun, write a **P** in the blank. If it's an adjective, write **A** and draw an arrow to the noun it modifies.

Examples: ___ *Both* boys ran. → _A_ *Both* boys ran.
___ *Both* are nice. → _P_ *Both* are nice.

1. ____ He took *that* to school.

2. ____ *Which* key fits into that lock?

3. ____ Rachel took *some* cookies to her grandma.

4. ____ I think that *those* are mine.

5. ____ *Whose* might be the grand prize winner?

6. ____ *This* dinosaur bone was the best find on the dig.

7. ____ Does that woman have *any* musical instruments.

8. ____ *Many* of the flags will be flown in the morning.

9. ____ *What* is the name of this song?

10. ____ Do you know *what* color?

11. ____ Mari and Tamal brought *several*.

12. ____ *These* trees will grow tall in the sun.

13. ____ The professor didn't want *either* of the samples.

14. ____ *Neither* crocodile looks friendly to me.

15. ____ I don't know *which* one to choose.

Appositives
NOTES

Appositives

Directions: Write an appositive into each blank to complete the sentences.

Examples: Jupiter, _____, went to the park. →
             Jupiter, _my kangaroo_ ,went to the park.

1. Mrs. Madigan, _____, assigns a lot of homework.

2. I gave Enrique, _____, a new robot.

3. Our dad took us to our favorite place, _____.

4. The librarian loaned Mr. McGuffin, _____, a book from the library.

5. Dashiell, _____, won the helicopter race.

6. After dinner, we went to Scoops, _____, for dessert.

7. Kitana threw the object, _____, at the tree.

8. Her goal is to travel to Antarctica, _____.

9. My mom and my Uncle Fernando, _____, grew up in Jackson Hole, Wyoming.

10. His new robot loaned Bleep Blorp, _____, a wrench.

11. The famous artist, _____, loved life.

12. Shadowbringer, _____, was a magical artifact.

Appositives

Directions: Write an appositive into each blank to complete the sentences.

Examples: Gus gave Mr. Bean, _____, a gift.   ➔
            Gus gave Mr. Bean, _his favorite comedian_, a gift.

1. We invited Sing and Raya, _____, to the beach.

2. Have you been to California, _____?

3. The mountain lion took her prey, _____, to her den for her babies.

4. My sister gave me a rose, _____, for my first day.

5. His favorite video game, _____, is on sale tomorrow.

6. Our pet penguin, _____, is a world champion.

7. Take this gift, _____, to our new neighbors.

8. Bob, _____, drove to the construction site.

9. For a field trip, my class went to an awful place, _____.

10. The visiting space alien, _____, loves blueberries.

11. They went camping in a very strange place, _____, with their computer club.

12. Abraham Lincoln, _____, is a famous American.

Appositives

Directions: Using the appositive, take the two sentences that are given, and rewrite them as a single sentence. **remember your commas**

Examples: She saw condors in Peru. Condors are huge birds.
→ She saw condors, *huge birds,* in Peru.

1. Maya Angelou appeared on television. Ms. Angelou is a famous author.

_____

_____

2. Grandpa cooked us fried fish. Fried fish is my favorite food.

_____

_____

3. Are you going to the celebration? The celebration is a birthday party.

_____

_____

4. Gael bought a new bike. Gael is Anita's brother.

_____

_____

5. We went to see a movie. The movie was a comedy masterpiece.

_____

_____

Appositives

Directions: Using the appositive, take the two sentences that are given, and rewrite them as a single sentence. **remember your commas**

Examples: Goober is a friend of mine. Goober is a swamp monster.
→ Goober, *a swamp monster*, is a friend of mine.

1. The rancher had to sell Trigger. Trigger was his favorite horse.

_____

_____

2. Sherlock solved the mystery in one minute. Sherlock is a great detective.

_____

_____

3. His mom and grandma made feta. Feta is a Greek cheese.

_____

_____

4. Mr. Hendrix is a music teacher. Mr. Hendrix became our principal.

_____

_____

5. She flew to Guam. Guam is an island in the Pacific Ocean.

_____

_____

Verbals
NOTES

Verbals

Directions: In the following sentences, circle any example of a <u>verbal</u>.

Examples: Hiking is very fun.   →   (Hiking) is very fun.
　　　　　　Dad likes to drive.　 →   Dad likes (to drive).

1. Robert has his favorite running shoes.

2. My grandfather likes to knit.

3. There is a new biking trail by our house.

4. Escaping was their only thought.

5. The jumping frog landed in my lap.

6. Her favorite thing is to swim In the river.

7. Crying babies are unpleasant in an airplane.

8. Their first attempt to fly ended with failure.

9. To succeed would be a dream.

10. The broken vase lay on the floor.

11. That poster has a picture of a lost dog.

12. To scale the mountain was his goal.

13. It was peaceful near the babbling brook.

14. Tobias was punished for cheating.

15. My favorite animal was the hopping kangaroo.

Verbals

Directions: In the following sentences, circle any example of a verbal. In the blank, write whether the verbal is an infinitive, a participle, or a gerund.

Examples: Running is a sport. _____

→ (Running) is a sport. ___*gerund*___

1. The teacher called my playing brilliant. _____

2. Her goal at the carnival was to win. _____

3. We loved the dancing chicken. _____

4. Those students like to help. _____

5. The screaming fan was very loud. _____

6. That donkey's braying hurt my ears. _____

7. To laugh seemed rude. _____

8. I gave her a thank you in writing. _____

9. Mom's new puppy just wanted to play. _____

10. A charming emcee hosted the show. _____

11. For most birds, flying is fundamental. _____

12. My Aunt Ursula loves to sail. _____

13. Reading is an important skill. _____

14. The cook picked up the broken kettle. _____

15. Our laughing monster won the contest. _____

Verbals

Directions: In the following sentences, circle any example of a <u>verbal</u>. In the blank, write whether the verbal is an <u>infinitive</u>, a <u>participle</u>, or a <u>gerund</u>.

    Examples: There is a cracked window. _____

    →   There is a (cracked) window. ___*participle*___

1. Our horses like to run. _____

2. The crawling baby was fast. _____

3. Drawing was my favorite hobby. _____

4. The counselor likes to help. _____

5. That man's singing sounded terrible. _____

6. My new friend had a worn coat. _____

7. To refuse was not an option. _____

8. His favorite sport is jousting. _____

9. Margot's grown children live in California. _____

10. Her cat just wanted to sleep. _____

11. That man in red is a boring speaker. _____

12. The team practiced running on Monday. _____

13. To learn was their only goal. _____

14. Our excited fans waited outside our hotel. _____

15. I think that coloring is my favorite hobby. _____

www.ingramcontent.com/pod-product-compliance
Lightning Source LLC
Chambersburg PA
CBHW060528010526
44110CB00052B/2533